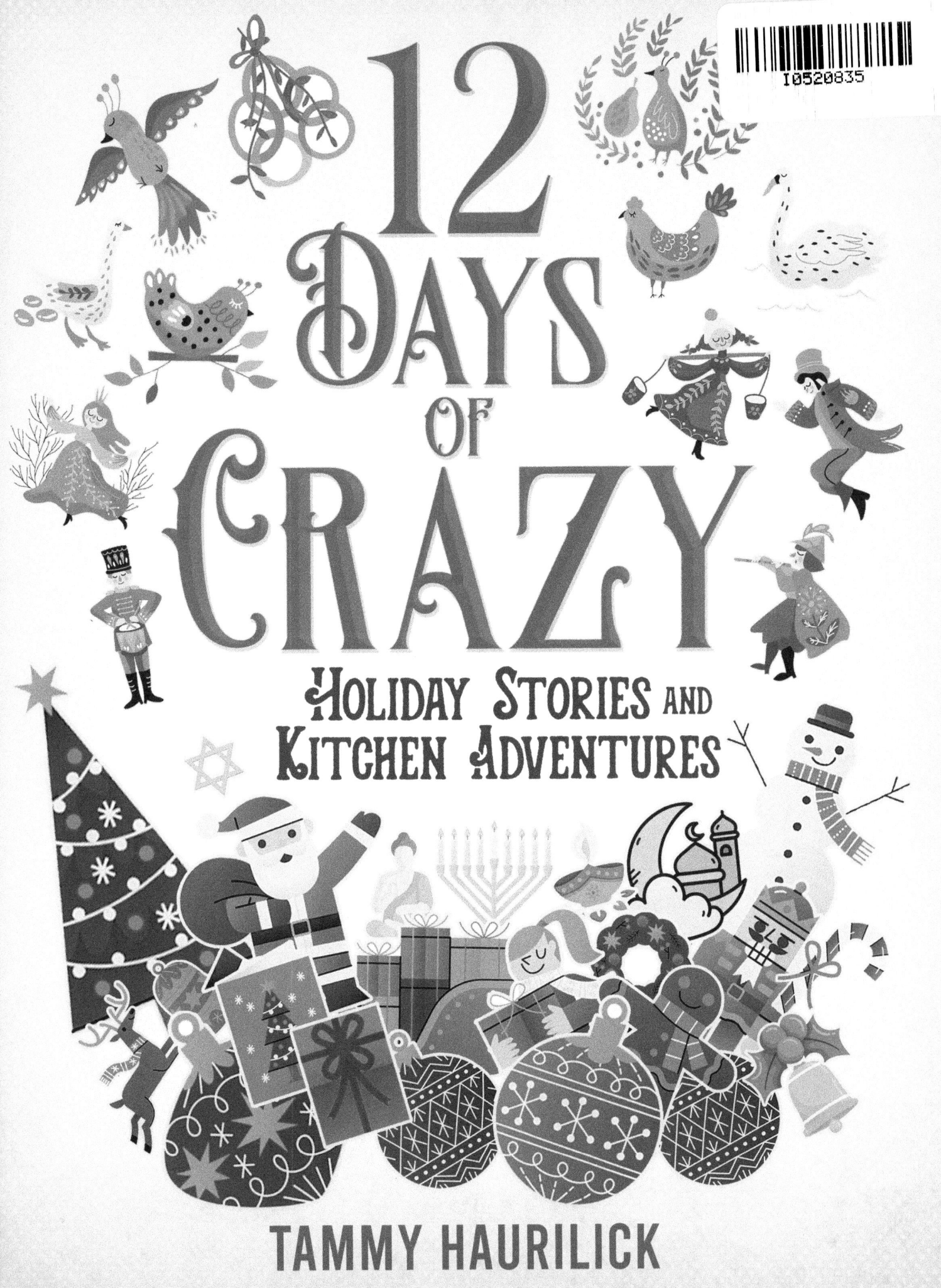

12 Days of Crazy

Holiday Stories and Kitchen Adventures

TAMMY HAURILICK

12 Days of Crazy
Holiday Stories and Kitchen Adventures
Tammy Haurilick
2023© by Tammy Haurilick
All rights reserved. Published 2023.

Printed in the United States of America
Spirit Media and our logos are trademarks of Spirit Media

✸ SPIRIT MEDIA
www.spiritmedia.us
1249 Kildaire Farm Rd STE 112
Cary, NC 27511
1 (888) 800-3744

Books › Christian Books & Bibles ›
Christian Living › Holidays › Christmas

Paperback ISBN: 978-1-961614-82-6
Audiobook ISBN: 978-1-961614-93-2
eBook ISBN: 978-1-961614-81-9
Library of Congress Control Number: 2023918819

"To my mother and father, Cathy and David, who taught me to appreciate and explore the world."

Waes Hael

Foreword

uilt is the ghost of morality past and we have a hell of a haunting going on here in America today. Everyone is feeling guilty about the commercialism of their holidays and how materialistic we as a civilization have become. Well, news flash, folks. We are NOT the first to bemoan the lack of spirituality. Far from it, in fact. From Ancient Roman times, with Seneca the Younger C.E. 50 to Silvae, then to Cromwell in the Restoration Period of 1642-1660, and yet even further still to the late 1800s in the new America, each and every one of these societies tried to restrict the celebration of Christmas/Winter Solstice in some form or fashion.

Those were some crazy days. Twelve crazy days, in fact, that began with a celebration that lasted several months, but due to the constant complaints of those more pious than most, eventually ended up as a twelve-day celebration. This was borrowing a tradition from the Egyptians, who modeled their original twelve-day festival of Horus after their agricultural calendar. In Egypt, extravagant parties were held to celebrate the rebirth of Horus that lasted a full twelve days with ceremonies welcoming the sun and praising the light.

When the Babylonians became aware of this celebration, they held one of their own, honoring their own creator/**sun** god; Marduk. They called this celebration Zagmak and they believed that Marduk was the creator who made the world one of peace, order and beauty.

In pre-Christian times, it was a twelve-day celebration of light and harvest, and family and food. Focusing on the harvest, and preparing for the new year to come, it also became a community event where villages and people from different parts of the country came together to share in the bounty of the fall. It served a dual purpose as well: as the social networking apparatus of the time, news was passed along from relatives in different towns, marriages arranged and performed and business conducted. With no other means of communication other than letters or word of mouth, these get-togethers played a vital role in the Society. Each day was celebrated individually for its own reason, but overall, the whole of the festival was focused on togetherness and relaxing, enjoying what they managed to harvest for the winter and making plans for the spring.

When Christianity came about, the days became named for various Saints or religious events. Christmas Day itself was a day first venerated by the Pagans as the day of the Birth of the Unconquered Sun. To get more converts to Christianity, the Church merely used a play on words, turning the Birth of the **Sun** into the Birth of the **Son**. It was just that simple of an idea to appropriate the day, change the spelling of the name of the deity being celebrated and then let the church do its work at spreading the new story.

In return for assuring a good turnout at the Celebration of the Savior's birth, the Church turned a blind eye toward the populace celebrating the Holiday as it had always been celebrated. Remember, **NOWHERE** in the Bible does it give a specific date for the birth of Christ. The day was chosen in 325 A.D. at the Council of Nicea, where the Bishop of Myra was present (Saint Nicholas).

Late December festivities are deeply rooted in popular culture, both in observance of the Winter Solstice and in celebration of leisure and plenty of agricultural societies. The church elders at the time came to the conclusion that if they couldn't get the populace to convert, then they would have THEIR feast day on the same day as the Pagan's and get them in there eventually, sideways. Sort of a "if we build it, they will come" theory (homage to Kevin Costner!!). Again, a tradition was born out of what once was quite an ordinary, regular day.

Back to the overall downsizing of the celebration from lasting several months to a mere twelve days. Again, the most religious of the time complained mightily about the excesses of the day:

From Seneca the younger—from the Epistolae around 50 A.D.:

"It is now the month of December, when the greatest part of the city is in a bustle. Loose reins are given to public dissipation; everywhere you may hear the sound of great preparations, as if there were some real difference between the days devoted to Saturn and those for transacting business… Were you here, I would willingly confer with you as to the plan of our conduct; whether we should behave in our usual way, or, to avoid singularity, both take a better supper and throw off the toga."

From the English Restoration in 1644:

"Specific penalties were to be imposed on anyone found holding or attending a special Christmas church service, it was ordered that shops and markets were to stay open on 25 December, the Lord Mayor was repeatedly ordered to ensure that London stayed open for business on 25 December, and when it met on 25 December 1656 the second Protectorate Parliament discussed the virtues of passing further legislation clamping down on the celebration of Christmas (though no Bill was, in fact, produced)."

As Cotton Mather from the Americas put it in 1687, which his son, Increase Mather also commented on the same in 1712:

"The generality of Christmas-keepers observe that festival after such a manner as is highly dishonourable to the name of Christ. How few are there comparatively that spend those holidays (as they are called) after a Holy manner. But they are consumed in Compotations, in Interludes, in playing at cards, in revellings, in excess of Wine, in Mad Mirth..."

I have worn my copy of the book "The Battle for Christmas" by Stephen Nissenbaum, a Pulitzer finalist book and a fantastic read, which mentions about how Christ's Nativity was celebrated:

"The Feast of Christ's Nativity is spent in Reveling, Dicing, Carding, Masking (see Saturnalia and role reversal) and in all Licentious Liberty by Mad Mirth, by Long Eating, by Hard Drinking, by Lewd Gaming, by Rude Reveling…"

In 1659, in the Massachusetts Bay Colony, they made it illegal to observe the holiday in public. It was declared during this time that *"whosoever shall be found observing any such day as Christmas or the like, either by forbearing of labor, feasting, or any other way"* will be levied a 5 shilling fine. The law lived a short life and was repealed in 1681 under pressure from London.

In 1850, Harriet Beecher Stowe wrote in one of her novels:

"Christmas is coming in a fortnight, and I have got to think up presents for everybody!! Dear me, it's so tedious!"

And let's also remember that the holiday time frame has been whittled down from lasting several months, starting in late November and going to Candlemas on February 2nd, to a mere twelve days of Christmas, modeled after the Egyptian Agricultural calendar.

Guess what else? All holidays are made up.

Yup. You heard me. All holidays are fabrications, inventions of time and tradition, boredom and banality. For the people who like to put down Christmas, Kwanzaa, and other holidays as made up and basically say they have no validity... this is what I will say to you. **Every holiday**, including Christmas, was once just a plain old ordinary day until someone or several someones got together and decided that this day above all others, needed to be recognized. Christmas wasn't Christmas until the Council

at Nicea in 325 A.D. That's where we got the Nicene Creed from and where all who attended decided that Jesus' Birthday should be celebrated on December 25th.

The one uniting factor behind all holidays is the need to be with other like-minded people. Be it religion, family, or just the need for human contact, people will find a way and a reason to get together to eat, talk, and just be with one another for human companionship.

Many cultures the world over perform solstice ceremonies. At the base of these ceremonies is the idea that the Sun would never return unless humans intervened with vigil or frantic celebration. Sort of a pray-up-the-sun and sing-down-the-moon ideology. And perhaps, our impulse to hold onto certain traditions today—candles, evergreens, feasting and generosity—are echoes of a past that extends many thousands of years further than we ever before imagined.

Winter solstice was overlaid with Christmas, and the observance of Christmas spread throughout the globe. Along the way, we lost some of the history of our celebrations, a lot of the history actually, to a single seasonal event. Many people—of many different beliefs—are looking to regain that connection now. Which is why I really wanted to write this book, to put the history out there about the song, "Twelve Days of Christmas" and to revive some old, old traditions of Winter Solstice of various cultures and maybe get people back to celebrating them, for whatever reasons suit them best.

Please understand, my intent is NOT to make a definitive statement of the origins of the song, or on the cultures involved, NOR as a sort of final opinion on the religions involved either. Rather, my aim is short and simple. I am going to show the history of one of the most endearing songs of the Season and perhaps remember and revive some pretty interesting and ancient traditions, while also adding a few new, multi-cultural additions.

It's official. Hell has frozen over and I wore flip-flops to the party!! Let me tell you an interesting story that begins with yet another clichéd first line that will quickly (VERY quickly, I assure you) degenerate into a long and detailed story of how I kept myself sane (did too, Dad—back off!) while I spent a year in an Iraqi prison. Inside the wire and heavily armed, but in a prison nonetheless. It was simultaneously the worst year of my life and the greatest blessing that God has ever given me, and I was gifted with that realization in a single moment. That moment occurred when (here comes another clichéd line—wait for it . . .)

"It was a dark and stormy night" in a remote corner of Iraq, the night hell froze over. It was two in the morning or so, sometime in February during the rainy season (who knew? a rainy season in Iraq) and it was so cold that for thirty minutes that dark, windy, wet and miserable pre-dawn morning, for the first time in sixty years, there was snow in southern Iraq.

It only lasted a scant half hour and then it went back to the bone numbing cold rain that turned the dirt and sand surrounding my guard tower into the most heavy-ain't-coming-off-no-how-no-way-

is-this-night-EVER-going-to-end mud on your boots ever! Each boot would be quickly coated with this sludge, dry, and then solidify. Then it would attract another layer of mud on your next roving watch, called a Dorea (Door-Ree-Ah) in Arabic, until you literally had feet of clay. I weighed my boots one night after work, just for giggles, and they weighed a whopping fifteen pounds! I figured it to be two pounds boots and thirteen pounds clay.

During the course of the rainy Season that winter, I went through two pairs of boots. That red mud could suck the soul right out of you. Putting one foot in front of the other was not a cheery little song from Rudolph the Red-nosed Reindeer Christmas special but a mantra to be chanted over and over. Anything to get you around the corner and onto the brown mile, where you were guaranteed to find a few solid spots, a few moments of relief. I came away from my year in the country with many things (aside from sand everywhere!!), among them kick-ass calves from the mud, and tight-ass (no pun intended) glutes from NEVER, and I mean NEVER, letting my sit-upon sit upon the toilet seats in the port-a-potties on the Theatre Internment Facility (TIF) or the Forward Operating Base (FOB). Picture a port-a-potty in 145°F heat after consuming 15-20 bottles of water during a shift, and you will get an understanding of the squatting power you can attain.

Wait a minute!! This book was supposed to be about the twelve days of Christmas and its history; when will she get around to writing about that? Wait for it, friends. Another thing I learned over there is the value of patience and that sometimes too much information (TMI) can work to your benefit. During the course of this writing, I will occasionally hitchhike off on a tangent that might not seem relevant at the time but will make sense and become pertinent when the time is right. I promise.

Let's return to the clichéd story already in progress. It was a dark and stormy night in a remote corner of Iraq. It was two in the morning or so and I was in my guard tower, staring in complete bewilderment at my outstretched gloved hand that was currently covered in snow. I held my hand up to the light to see the flakes glisten in the sharp air and to simultaneously keep a peripheral eye on the yard below. I usually took my turn in the tower first watch, the zero to four watch. It was quiet, peaceful, little action in the yard, and you could gather your thoughts and think things over. Picture Winnie the Pooh, with his little butterscotch paw, tapping his forehead and going "think, think, think".

Now picture him doing that wearing Kevlar and carrying an M16 with an M203 grenade launcher, and you have me, in my tower at Delta Quad at two in the morning, or thereabouts. Humming a little hum, thinking some minor thinks, and keeping an eye out for individuals considering enrollment in the self-release program at Camp Bucca (that's escaping to you mere civilians). I started humming the song the twelve days of Christmas and you know how it is when you get a song in your head? Well, try getting one in your head early in the morning with nothing to do but watch an empty yard for four hours!!! It gets you thinking. And I thought, I want to learn more about this song and where it came from. And I thought to myself, when I get off work, I will go and research some at the computer lab at the Liberty Lounge and see what's what.

So, after my shift that morning, I googled the song. The more I read about it, the more I became interested in where this song about a Mid-Winter Festival originated and what it was truly about. I also became interested in the Mid-Winter Festivals of other cultures. Every one of them, it seemed, revolved around (pun intended) the **Sun**, Winter Solstice, and Rebirth. Every story I read, every article, every person I talked to led to yet another tidbit of information to be followed up on. So, I invite you to come along and see what I found out, read my opinions, random thoughts and postulations about why things happened the way they did.

Agree or disagree with me, vehemently shout your disapproval from the rooftops. But before you do, read all the books listed in the bibliography and visit all the websites and become more informed about some of these unbelievably interesting celebrations. The world is so much smaller than we can possibly imagine and yet at the same time so wonderfully immense and diverse.

When you are trying to write a book or a webpage, and let's face it, it's all trying here, you try for a killer opening first line. I wanted one that would tie the two most important aspects of this book together, which are:

1. The story of the 12 Days of Christmas.

2. HOW I came up with the idea for it and where.

The HOW and WHERE I came up with the idea and started researching it are as equally important as the locale was integral to the why I tried to add the multicultural factor as accurately as possible. I wanted to make it as multicultural as possible because my year in Iraq changed my worldview forever. I met the people of Iraq, the "real" people of Iraq and they changed me, for the better, I hope. I have never met a more generous and giving group of people. It seemed the less they had, the more they invited you to come and share with them.

The Iraqi guards we worked with and were, in theory, training to do the job, ate separately from us. They were fed the same meals as the detainees; the food came on the same trucks and every morning, at 0-dark-thirty when breakfast arrived, we guards would hunker down in our respective shacks and eat. The Iraqi contingent ate boiled eggs wrapped in buttered flatbread and drank hot sweet chai. We ate nasty, cold, fried things driven in from the chow hall. Everything that chow sent us was fried and greasy and, by the time it reached us. . .cold.

After a while, I gave up on breakfast and just ate two cups of cereal and a glass of milk. Before too long, however, the Iraqi guards started asking us to come sit with them on their porch and try a boiled egg with flatbread. Or a bottle of hot chai (we used recycled water bottles that crackled and popped from numerous uses). The chai was like Southern sweet tea times ten, only not. Better food, interesting people, tentative friendships and some really, really cool stories all came together those cool mornings (and later, really hot mornings) sharing breakfast with our Iraqi counterparts. It was

really addictive, sweet tea and boiled eggs, and I have yet to have butter that tasted as sweet.

I had to find out more about them and to add to this whole story, if they had a winter celebration too. Well in fact, they do, but it's a moveable feast, it changes every year, but you will read about their memories of Ramadan and Eid in the Memories section of this book. In the course of finding out about Iraqi culture, I investigated other cultures and countries, and in doing so, decided to share what I found out with you. On each day of the twelve days of Christmas, there will be a different culture section. So while you can maybe sing a song, or cook a meal that is pertinent to that particular day of Christmas, you can also bake/cook/create something from another culture's winter celebration.

If there are errors in the data, please chalk them up to the unbelievably numerous sources available (see bibliography) and the innumerable opinions of the various authors, individuals and religious leaders I interviewed (over 200) and my own humble opinion. If you find errors, I am sorry, there are centuries-worth of data to pile through. If there are inconsistencies, well, it's ancient history so it's FULL of inconsistencies. It's sort of the standard. If you don't like the book in general, tough. Write your own book.

Introduction

et's move into the actual history of the twelve days. Not only the song, but the actual festival for which it is named. The twelve days of Christmas begins on Christmas day and finishes up on the Eve of Epiphany on January 5th, the Feast of Epiphany being on January 6th. Here, historians are divided as to the true origins of the song, some say it dates back to English origins in the early 1500s, others are firm in their conviction that it is French in origin. What is an absolute fact is that it first appeared in the written form in 1780 in a book called "Mirth Without Mischief." In several portions of the lyrics, words are used that are French in origin. In the fifth verse, "Five Golden Rings," the gold rings refer to the gold-necked pheasant, which wasn't introduced to England until the 1770s; so there are arguments for both sides.

Now, I have always loved the song "The Twelve Days of Christmas" So, a few days after that pretty momentous night, I went and googled it and Holy cow!!! What results!! That's where I learned about the debate over its actual origins. It's either a cute counting song dating back to before the Reformation of the Church in England (Y'know, Cromwell and the Roundheads....Cromwell, by the way, DID NOT kill Christmas) or a hidden way to teach the catechism. Most of my sources disprove the hidden catechism idea, the general theory seems to be it's just a pleasant counting song and/or a drinking game played at the holiday time.

They (the ubiquitous THEY) state that the ideas that some would theorize were being taught in secret were openly taught in church at the time anyway, so why would there be a need for a hidden code to remember these tenets of belief? Anyway, I started reading about the song and Mid-Winter Solstice, and it amazed me how many cultures throughout the world have a midwinter celebration of some sort.

Of course, they are called by many different names and have different reasoning (religious or otherwise) behind their being, but they all have one basic theme in common. They are celebrations of hope and light, of family and love, of winter being at the half mark and spring moving into view. I find it comforting that with all the religious debate and confrontation in the world that there is this universal ancient idea—winter solstice—that holds true to almost every major religion and culture, and that these celebrations aren't just an invention of the ancient Europeans. They are everywhere.

Let's lay out an ancient civilization timeline as a visual aid, okay? Sort of a "which came first, the chicken or the egg" situation. Also keep in mind that as many books as you pick up will reflect as many different dates listed for the start of any one of these "official" holidays. Just like the birth of Jesus Christ, name a date that you consider the official date of Christ's birth and there is probably some literature or some learned professor somewhere that can support that date with reams of knowledge and references.

My point in laying out a timeline is to show a simple progression of where the ideas may have come from, and how they might have moved across the globe and across time, through the simple act of exploration and cultural expansion. (Okay, exploration and a lot of battles, overthrowing countries and kings, pillaging and conquering, that sort of thing)

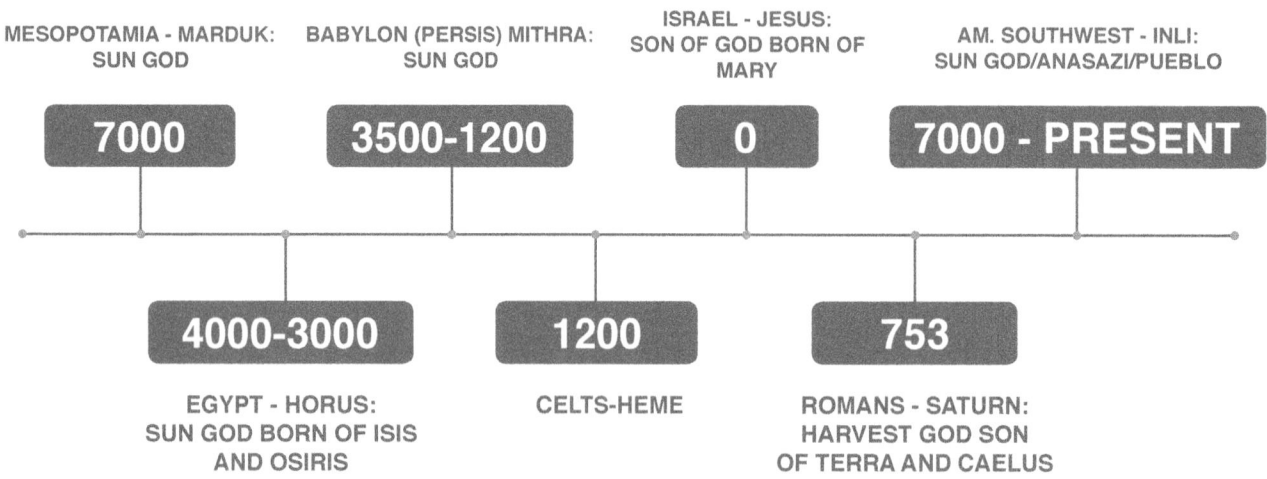

1 - Let's begin with Mesopotamia, The Fertile Crescent, the birthplace of ALL civilization. This civilization dates back as far as 7,000 years. That place, that particular culture can be listed as the fore-runner of most all other civilizations we as a human race are aware of. The ancient god of Mesopotamia AND Babylonia, was most notably, Marduk, the God of the Sun.

2 - Then we have the Egyptians, coming in at about 3,000 to 4,000 years ago. The mid-winter festival of the ancient Egyptians celebrated the birth of Horus, son of Isis (the divine mother-goddess). The festival lasted twelve days, reflecting their twelve-month calendar. This is where a lot of scholars believe the root for the twelve days of Christmas celebration began, both as a festival and as a cultural/religious event.

3 - Next on our line up are the Greeks, taking position from 3,500 years ago to about 1,200 years ago.

4 - Here we have the Celts making their presence known with their gods and practices. The most well known of these gods is Herne, or the Green Man.

5 - It's zero hour!! The time where all dates are sprung from, year zero, the birth of Jesus Christ. In 325 A.D., Emperor Constantine (First Christian emperor) convened the Council of Nicea in what is now present day Turkey. This was the origination of the Nicene Creed, the belief in the Holy Trinity. church leaders proclaimed the twelve days from December 25th to January 5th, the Eve of Epiphany as a sacred, festive season. In fact, research has brought to light the theory that the Christians also moved the day of the celebration of Christ's birth to the 25th of December in order to help move along the conversion of Pagans and other religions. Hey, they must have figured, if they come to the party, they might listen to the spiel. Kind of like those timeshare weekends that companies offer, y'know, where you agree to listen to a sales pitch for a timeshare in Walla Walla Wherever in exchange for a weekend of fun and frivolity. Sort of a "If you build it, they will come" theory (homage to Kevin Costner !!!)

Believe that information or not, there is significant evidence to prove that that is precisely what the Christian leaders of the day did.

A fascinating book *"Holy Blood, Holy Grail"* by Michael Baigent, Richard Leigh, and Henry Lincoln discusses the pragmatic political motives of the fourth-century Roman emperor Constantine, who first moved the celebration of Christmas to December 25th. The authors claim that Constantine followed the cult of Sol Invictus, a monotheistic form of sun worship that originated in Syria and was imposed by Roman emperors on their subjects a century earlier.

"His primary, indeed obsessive, objective was unity—unity in politics, in religion, and in territory. A cult or state religion that included all other cults within it obviously helped to achieve this objective. In the interests of unity, Constantine deliberately chose to blur the distinctions among Christianity, Mithraism (another Sun cult of the time) and Sol Invictus."

That's why Constantine decreed that Sunday—"the venerable day of the sun" would be the official day of rest. (Early Christians before then celebrated their holy day on the Jewish Sabbath—Saturday.)

That's also why, by his edict, the book claims—the celebration of Jesus' birthday was moved from January 6th (Epiphany today) to December 25th, celebrated by the cult of Sol Invictus as Natilis Invictus, the rebirth of the sun. There is also a long standing theory that many of the most ancient cathedrals and places of worship were actually first Pagan temples and that the Christians co-opted the locations as well as the days of pagan religious events. Another theory is that ancient cathedrals have carvings in them that are in fact monuments to pagan gods, further supporting their assertion that old cathedrals were at first Pagan in origin.

The book "The Sun in the Church" by J. L. Heilbron, claims that many of the ancient cathedrals are in fact, observatories, used to track the movements of the sun. It is a very intense and interesting read, way too thinky for me (my brain imploded in chapter four with a complex algebraic equation) but I recommend it to anyone who wishes to pursue that avenue of interest further, (confused yet? don't be! I have many, many more pages with which to do that yet).

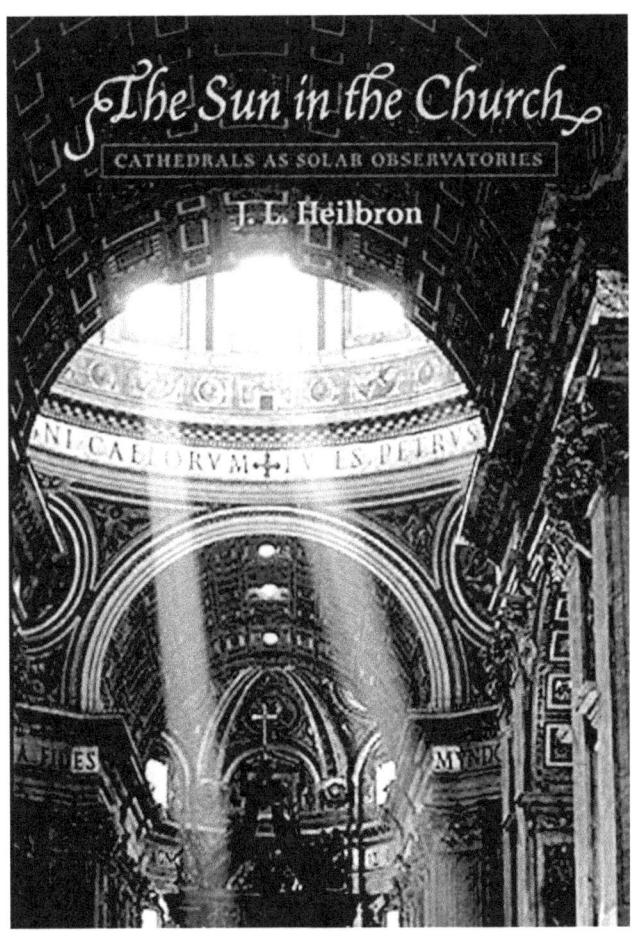

6 - Now of course, the Romans entered the picture about 2,000 years ago, taking over Egypt, installing their own beliefs, and incorporating the Egyptians beliefs into their own. Their belief system at the time celebrated the god of the Harvest/god of the Seed, Saturn, at Solstice time at a festival known as Saturnalia. During this festival, which lasts from December 17th to December 24th, the main feature was the role reversal of society. Men could dress up as women and women as men, servants had freedoms that were normally forbidden them the rest of the year. Masters would at times serve the servants. Parties went on from sunup to sundown. Excess was the norm, which is not surprising for the Roman culture that is known for not only its excesses but its solid preparation and adulation to excess. These are the people who built a special building that withstood the hardships of over 2,000 plus years so we could stumble upon it and figure out what it was built for. These folks built a Vomitorium. Yup. You read correctly. A Vomitorium, a building designed and built especially for the sole purpose of being able to vomit in comfort so as to return to the Feast to gorge some more. You really have to admire a culture that places that much forethought on one event. Icky. Impressive, but icky. They also liked to drink to excess and had a god for that express purpose by the name of Bacchanalia, the god of Wine. They also lived to do most things naked. The Olympics were done naked, most sports, a lot of parties, a lot of their festivals, and quite a few of their religious events. Very single minded folks, the Romans.

7 - Next to last on the timeline and one of the most ancient are the Chacoans, ancestors to the Anasazi. The Anasazi are the ancestors to the modern day Pueblo Indians of the American Southwest.

18

Table of Contents

20

A PARTRIDGE IN A PEAR TREE

People have used fruit as symbols of men and women since Ancient times. For example an Apple for a male and a Pear for a female. The partridge is best known for perching in tress and was introduced to England in the 1770's.

People have used fruit as symbols of men and women since Ancient times. For example, an apple will symbolize a male and a pear will symbolize a female. The partridge is known for perching in trees and was introduced into England in the 1770s. The phrase "A Partridge in a Pear Tree" takes on a whole new perspective with that information. Lusty bunch, the medieval folks!

Also known as Boxing Day, St. Stephen's Day, and Wren's Day.

Boxing Day

Boxing Day is the traditional day in Britain for giving the servants their presents or yearly bonus. It was a day off for the working class, a day when the "Upper Crust" had to fend for themselves and the lower classes had their time for Christmas. There are as many different legends as to why this day began as there are days in the calendar.

It is NOT:

- A day for families to "Box" each other and work out the year's frustrations and pent-up aggression.

- Remove all the useless, now empty boxes from the house the day AFTER St. Nick visited.

- Nor has it anything to do with unwanted gifts, returns and re-gifting.

It is quite simply, the day after Christmas when the servants and working classes had THEIR Christmas and could be with their families and exchange gifts. Traditionally, the masters and the employers at this time would bestow the yearly stipend/gifts upon their servants/employees. That tradition gradually morphed into one where those who had more would give to those who had less. In present times, you could view it as the day the service industry would have the day off, so that employees of restaurants, retail and entertainment establishments could relax and be at home with their families too.

Feast of St. Stephen

Stephen was stoned to death (c. C.E. 34-35)

Stephen was one of the first seven Deacons in the Church. His whole life's story and the events that had him beatified can be found in the Acts of the Apostles. After Jesus' death, the Apostles had found that they needed helpers to look after the care of the widows and the poor. Stephen was one of the most successful of these deacons. He apparently was so eloquent and passionate in his preachings that many of his followers became followers of Jesus.

There was a division in the Church at this time between the Jews that spoke Greek and the Jews that spoke Aramaic. Stephen's enemies bribed men to say that Stephen was speaking blasphemous words against Moses and against God. The elders and the scribes were stirred up and brought him before the Sanhedrin, the supreme Jewish tribunal, which had authority in both civil and religious matters. Stephen defended himself well; however, at the conclusion of his defense he made a statement that did not do him any good:

"Yet not in houses made by hands does the Most High dwell, even as the prophet says . . . Stiffnecked and uncircumcised in heart and ear, you always oppose the Holy Spirit; as your father did, so do you also. Which of the prophets have not your fathers persecuted? And they killed those who foretold the coming of the Just One, of whom you have now been the betrayers and murderers, you who received the Law as an ordinance of angels and did not keep it." (Acts 6:11) (Acts 6:13-14).

Stephen's final speech was presented as accusing the Jews of persecuting prophets who spoke out against their sins. Angering his accusers to the point of no return, his honesty rewarded him with his death. The crowd could no longer contain their rage and they rushed him outside the gates of Jerusalem and stoned Stephen to death. Among the crowd was a young Jew named Saul of Tarsus who later became Paul the Apostle, "and Saul entirely approved of putting him to death." (Acts 8:1)

St. Stephen's Day is also a popular day for visiting family members.

Wren's Day

Some people believe the origin of Wren's Day may be a Samhain or midwinter sacrifice and/or celebration, as Celtic mythology considered the robin a symbol of the New Year and the wren a symbol of the old year. Most of the traditions involve killing a wren, as a symbolic "killing" or closing of the Old Year. Christians view Wren's Day as a sort of retribution as the legend goes that a wren betrayed St. Stephen by chattering away as he tried to hide from his enemies behind a bush.

That story may also have influenced Scandinavian settlers during the Viking invasions of the 8th-10th centuries. One of the numerous legends states that during one of the Viking raids in the 700s, a band of Irish soldiers were betrayed by a wren as they were sneaking up on a bunch of Vikings while at camp. The wren innocently began to eat bread crumbs left on the head of a drum and the resulting rat-a-tat-tat woke the camp which ultimately led to the Irish soldier's defeat.

One other country tradition is that young boys in the villages blacken their faces and become

"Wren Boys". They catch and kill a wren, or use a straw-stuffed representation of a bird, and parade around the village singing songs and asking for money to "bury the wren." The money collected is used to pay for the food and drink at the "Wren Dance" held that night.

A popular rhyme, known to many Irish children and sung at each house visited by the mummers, goes as follows:

The wren, the wren, the king of all birds,

On St. Stephen's Day was caught in the furze,

Up with the penny and down with the pan,

Give us a penny to bury the wren.

BIBLICAL INTERPRETATION

The Partridge in a Pear Tree symbolizes Jesus Christ.

he Partridge in a Pear tree symbolizes Jesus Christ.

26

ANOTHER CULTURE'S
WINTER CELEBRATION

Santa Claus
Dec 25

United States - Santa Claus and Christmas in Australia

The history of the figure we know as Santa Claus predates Christian history. He was first associated with the Winter Solstice and is known by a variety of names. The Green Man, Odin, and Herne are a few, but he was first and foremost a shaman, whose primary duties were to see to the proper observances of ritual designed to ensure the return of the sun. He oversaw the proper procedure for harvest time, and then the rituals of observing the shortest day of the year, and then again the procedures for springtime planting. Things had to be done correctly in order to NOT offend the gods, as the sun had to make its reappearance at Winter Solstice.

The days HAD to start getting longer, in order for the society whose lives revolved around agriculture, to have faith that they would see the spring again. It was the rebirth of a new year and a rebirth of life for them. Thousands of years ago, this was not all stuff and stories, told around a table or fire for amusement. This was their reality. Read a very interesting and detailed book called "When Santa was a Shaman" by Tony Van Rentgerghem, to get a more accurate and detailed account of his metamorphosis from shaman to happy elf.

In Australia, Christmas comes in the summer months, so there is NEVER a White Christmas. Christmas holidays are marked by trips to the beach, barbecues with the family and lounging by the swimming pool. The season is marked by the three S's: Sun, sand, and surfing!! Children are letting out from school, so there is the summer holiday to get excited about as well as Christmas. A favorite dessert well known at the holiday is something called "Pavlova" so named for a ballerina named Anna Pavlova who visited Perth in 1935. Chef Herbert Esplanade created a meringue treat for her and it is now a holiday favorite. Please read "Six White Boomers" by Rolf Harris and the song by the same name.

Word Knerd

Jesus and Horus similarities:

1. Both conceived of a virgin.

2. Horus' mother was Meri; Jesus' mother was Mary.

3. Horus' father was Jo-Seph and Jesus' father was Joseph.

4. The ancient Egyptians celebrated Horus' birth on December 21st or the winter solstice and Christians celebrate Jesus' Birthday on December 25th.

5. Jesus was visited by three Wise Men at birth and Horus was visited by three solar deities.

6. Neither Jesus nor Horus have a recorded history of their lives between ages 12-30; both were baptized at age thirty.

7. Both have twelve disciples.

8. Jesus is known as the Christ "anointed one" and Horus was known as KRST, also "anointed one."

9. Both are associated with the sign of Pisces, "the Fish," the beetle, the vine, and the shepherd.

10. Both were sent to Hell and resurrected in three days.

This information came from a book called "The World's Sixteen Crucified Saviors" by Kersey Graves. He actually has a total of forty-six comparisons, but I listed only ten. Take the time to go and read it, it's a very detailed and interesting read. While I don't agree with most of it, it does raise interesting questions.

Books

"Six White Boomers" with CD
by Rolf Harris
ISBN - 9781865046174

Hawaiian Night Before
Christmas by Carolyn Macy
ISBN - 9781589805989

Santa Claus and the Molokai
Mules by Jeffrey Garcia
(Author), Jamie Meckel
(Illustrator)
ISBN - 9780984094202

30

REMEMBRANCES

hese are the stories I collected from my friends, family and people I met while traveling overseas, most notably from the Coalition Forces in Camp Bucca, Iraq. These stories are their most favorite memories of their Winter Celebrations and Traditions.

The Christmas Tree Caper

David H.
(My dad, Christmas Aficionado Extraordinaire!!)

I grew up in rural Vermont. When I was about seventeen or eighteen, in the year 1959, my dad asked me to go up into the woods and cut the family Christmas tree. We could have gone to one of the various lots where trees were for sale but it was more fun and a lot less expensive to go out into the woods and find one. You know, like in the "olden days," or so we thought. In any case, I and one of my friends, Paul Shepard, drove up to the State Farm, a state property that encompassed the minimum security "farm" where prisoners worked growing crops and vegetables to feed not only themselves but other State institutions.

As Paul and I had hunted deer, squirrels and woodchucks on the state farm for many years, we were quite sure we could find a tree. Arriving at the selected area we spent several hours tramping through the snow looking for a suitable tree without success. They were too fat, too thin, too short, too tall, etc. Getting tired, we gave up and began the trek back to the car. But wait. Ahead of us, I could see a beautiful blue spruce pine tree. What a Christmas tree, the shape, the color, the thickness of the branches. It was like the good Lord had spent the past forty years sculpting this tree just for me. But what had caught my eye was the last seven feet of this tree. If the entire tree was not nice enough, the top was perfect. It was the type of tree that today you would pay a hundred dollars for, if you could find one that good. You know the tree that Currier and Ives paint or that ended up in the White House each year.

Well, what to do? I was enough of a tree hugger even back then to know that a true woodsman would not desecrate the forest by topping a tree. But, I was on a mission; my dad had sent me on a mission. One must not disappoint the family head. Besides, it was one tree, the woods were full of them. Who would know? Okay, so up the tree I went, carrying my small hand saw and hatchet. It took 10 to 15 minutes to work my way to the top. I can tell you, being forty feet up in a tree is a whole lot scarier than you think. I "guesstimated" about where to make my cut and Paul, standing below, suggested I drop down another foot or so to make sure. You know the old carpenter's saying "Measure twice, cut once." So, I started. Due to my having to hold on with one hand and cut with the other, it took me the better part of half an hour with that little saw, but the top came off and dropped down to the ground.

As we dragged the tree back to the car, I recall looking back at the once beautiful tree and thinking I had done a terrible thing. Somehow the Good Lord, or Smokey the Bear, would extract a measure of revenge in due course.

Okay, the deed done, we drove back to the house where we trimmed the bottom of the tree to fit the old family Christmas tree holder. At that point, my dad came home from work, took one look

at the tree, looked at me and said, "You topped a tree, didn't you?" He had spent many years in the woods himself, especially as a young man my age, working at the 1930s CCC camps on Mount Ascutney. He knew trees and logging, and had, in his day, probably cut down dozens just like the one I had mangled. I had to confess as there was no fooling him and I knew it. However, all I got from him was a disapproving look and a "don't do that again" comment as we carried the tree into the house. This was 1959 and money was tight. He wasn't about to tell me to take the tree back. So the old Depression era mentality kicked in. "Use it up, wear it out, make do or do without." That, plus what's done is done.

I am pretty sure that's the best Christmas Tree we ever had.

Guy Fawkes Night or Bonfire Night

Cathy H.
(my MUM!!!) Blantyre, Scotland

Every November 5th, children and adults celebrate the "November 5th, 1605 plot" to blow up the houses of Parliament. Guy Fawkes was hired by a bunch of unhappy Catholics to blow up the Protestant King and House of Parliament. Guy was betrayed, captured and burned at the stake. Very unlucky fellow. Anyways, when I was a wee lassie we used to go in the evenings after school with neighborhood friends and try to collect money for fireworks. We would either use a parent's garden cart or build our own, then make a guy (Fawkes) out of straw, or old pillow cases stuffed with rags, painted on face and dressed up in an assortment of men's old clothing. Then we would drag this work of art around the streets and sing "Penny for the guy, Penny for the guy, Who will give us a Penny for the guy."

We would knock on doors, and visit local shops, etc., and show off our great guy; he was definitely a much finer guy than the ones across the street. And, that's how we raised the money for fireworks. It was usually the adults, older kids, or teens who collected the junk and wood for the bonfires, then on the big night they would pick out the best guy and put him on top of the bonfire and light it up and set off the fireworks. If I remember correctly, after the fire got going, we could all throw our not-so-great guys onto the fire. Everybody would go home covered in smoke from the bonfire with all our clothes smelling of old wood and firecrackers.

There, aren't you proud of me?

Another holiday story from mum:

When I was about seven years old, I discovered there was no SANTA CLAUS. In my family, we always celebrated Christmas Day. Christmas Eve was last-minute food preparation and Midnight Mass at St. Joseph's Chapel. This year, my parents bought me a big pram for my double-jointed baby doll from last Christmas. The pram was too big to hide in the house, as was the custom in Christmas past.

This year, my folks had the pram stored with my Aunt Martha and Uncle John Madden, who lived about two miles from us. While we were at Midnight Mass, it started to snow and we had a bit of trouble getting home. Consequently, my aunt and uncle could not deliver the pram.

On Christmas morning, as we were walking in deep snow to my aunt's house to pick up my pram that Santa had delivered there in error, the penny dropped. Not only did I have to watch my brother Bill open his toys while we waited for the weather to clear, I froze my tush off helping my dad carry the pram through the snow back home and realized that Santa was my Dad.

Love you my angel, Mum.

RECIPES

ere I add recipes for the day: Both traditional and from different countries/cultures. I hope that you will try a few of these recipes and perhaps incorporate them into your family traditions.

Boxty

Now, Boxty is an Irish potato cake, rather like the Irish equivalent of a Jewish Latke or an American Hash Brown. The main difference is that you can thin it down to crepe consistency and wrap it around beef medallions with a gravy for Beef Boxty. When I looked online for a simple recipe for Boxty, I got inundated with dozens of very complicated recipes. But, seeing as how it is such a simple and versatile idea, I streamlined it for you. You can either make it the traditional way OR you can make a few in advance and use it as the "crust" for Shepherd's Pie (see below). So, with all that being said:

Ingredients

- 1½ cups grated raw potatoes
- 1 cup all purpose flour
- 1 cup leftover mashed potatoes
- 1 egg
- salt and pepper to taste
- ¼ cup olive oil

Directions

In a bowl, mix the grated potatoes and flour. Blend in the mashed potatoes.

In another bowl, whisk together the egg, milk, and seasonings. Mix in with the potato mixture. Shape into little patties about four inches across.

Heat olive oil in a large skillet over medium heat. Drop in patties and fry until golden brown. Drain on a paper towel-lined plate. Serve warm.

OR

Keep warm on a plate in the oven and use as a top for your Shepherd's Pie.

Shepherd's Pie

Now, I am a first-generation immigrant, born to a Scottish mother and a Russian father. Potatoes figure heavily in both cultures. Yay!! Here is a comfort food to beat all comfort foods as it IS actually good for you because it has other vegetables in it besides potatoes (okay, two more, but still).

Ingredients

- 1½ pounds hamburger
- 4 carrots, peeled and chopped
- 1 medium-sized onion, peeled and diced
- 6 medium-sized potatoes, boiled and mashed with butter and milk (about 2 1/4 cups when done)
- Salt and pepper to taste
- 1 beef bouillon cube (I use OXO)
- ½ cup boiling water
- 1 cup shredded Cheddar Cheese, (Cabot is best)

Directions

Brown the hamburger in a large skillet over medium high heat. Add diced onions. In a half cup of boiling water, dissolve the beef bouillon cube, and add it to the hamburger mixture. When browned and onions are translucent, remove from heat, drain, add in sliced carrots and set aside.

Place mixture in a 9x13 baking dish. Cover with mashed potatoes and sprinkle with shredded cheese. Bake in the oven at 350°F for 35–45 minutes or until carrots are soft.

The alternative is to use the Boxty patties from the first recipe and place it on top of the Shepherd's Pie. Sprinkle with cheese and bake at the same heat and time or until the carrots are soft.

Banoffee Pie

My mom and dad's next door neighbors are from Britain so of course, my Scottish mum made friends with them quickly. Claire has this awesome recipe for a dessert called Banoffee Pie that she served to us on Boxing Day for dinner at their house. It was funny because she brought out the pie and announced it like we were supposed to know what it was. We had no idea. She was surprised because she thought Banoffee Pie was an American invention. We assured her it was wholly a British thing and that we would try it anyway. Good thing we did. Eyes rolled back good!

Steve made his famous Bubble and Squeak that night. I tried to like it, I really did. Especially, since I have read about that particular recipe in numerous Bodice Rippers over the years. But the ONE thing they DIDN'T tell me in all those rip-tear-fondle-fondle books is that Bubble and Squeak's main ingredient is Brussel Sprouts. Not going to use that recipe here, if you are interested go to www.GourmetSleuth.com. But I will give you the Banoffee Pie recipe as it is very easy to make and has my second favorite flavor in the world in it: Toffee or caramel.

Ingredients

- Ready-made Graham Cracker crust

- 1 can of condensed milk

- Bunch of bananas

- Whipping Cream

- Chocolate (Flake)

- Coffee syrup of some sort (you can get Chocolate Flake, which is a Cadbury's product at World Market or any International Grocery store. If not, just shave some semi-sweet chocolate and use that. Same thing with the coffee syrup, I use Camp's Coffee, but if you can't find that, just use a half teaspoon of instant coffee with a tiny bit of water and THEN add it to the Cool Whip)

Directions

Boil the can of condensed milk for three hours in a big pot of water. Do NOT poke holes in the can. Make sure water covers the can at all times. Boiling it for three hours turns the condensed milk to a very rich toffee. Remove it from water after three hours, let it stand for four minutes. Use a towel to cover the can when you open it. Pour the toffee into the crust and spread evenly. Slice bananas into the crust and make it as thick as you want. Mix one teaspoon of Camp Coffee into the whipping cream and spread over top of the bananas, and put in the fridge to set for a while. Top with shaved chocolate or Chocolate Flake if you can get it.

Please, please, please, cover the can of Condensed milk with a towel when you open it. Claire's daughter has a nice little scar on her cheek from some boiling hot toffee as a learning memento when making the pie one year.

Pavlova

Pavlova is a traditional Australian dessert served at Christmas time. It was named after Anna Pavlova, the famous ballerina, after she visited Australia in the mid 1930s. A chef at the hotel where she was staying created the dessert especially for her. It is a sweet and light dessert, very easy to make, and fun to play around with as many variations of the recipe as there are fruits available to use. It is normally made in one large "cake", then spread with a fruit mixture, but you can also make small "meringue nests" or "cups" for individual servings.

There are numerous easy meringue recipes available online, or barring that, you can actually buy pre-made meringue nests. Go to www.vermontcountrystore.com and use the search term "meringue nests." Or call 1-800-776-5730 for direct service. The item number is No. 54362 in the catalog. The Vermont Country Store has unbelievably good service and the owners Lyman, Eliot, Cabot and Gardner Orton are Vermont Gorgeous!! Nice guys too. Another website I use is the www.buybritish.net/store, where you can get hard-to-find British food and sweet items. I buy the Meringue nests from them. If you buy the pre-mades, just use the fruit portion of any Pavlova recipe you can find. Make sure you serve immediately after making.

Ingredients

- 3 egg whites

- 1 pinch salt

- 1 cup white sugar

- 1 tablespoon cornstarch

- 1 teaspoon lemon juice

- 1 ¼ cups heavy whipping cream

- ½ cup confectioners sugar

- ½ tsp vanilla

- 1 pint fresh fruits, strawberries are best but use kiwis too for color

Directions

Preheat the oven to 300°F.

Line a cookie sheet with parchment paper. Draw a nine inch circle on paper with a pencil or several small four-inch circles.

In a bowl, beat egg whites with an electric mixer (or by hand if you want the exercise) until stiff peaks form. It should look soft and satiny. Add 3/4 cup of the sugar gradually, while continuing to whip the whites. Mix cornstarch with the remaining 1/4 cup of sugar and fold into the meringue. Then add the lemon juice and make sure it's well blended.

Spread the meringue to fit the nine-inch circle to about 1/4 inch thick OR using a pastry bag with a 3/4 inch star tip, pipe small meringue cups on the four-inch circles. Make the small cups about 2-3 inches high and don't forget to form a bottom.

Bake the meringue for about an hour. Turn off the oven and leave the meringue in for another thirty minutes. Meringues should be hard and crusty on the outside and soft and chewy on the inside.

In another bowl, mix the whipping cream with the vanilla and the half cup of confectioner's sugar. Whip until thick. Decorate the meringues with the fruit of your choice and top with whipped cream. I use Cool Whip myself and it tastes just as good as the homemade stuff, although my mum would disagree ☺.

Day 1

PUZZLES

Q D Y D R Y H Y W Z S P C J
D N O W Z E Y E C B E Y U E
F A O R P E O H O A T W G S
R L C E O D R X R P U D U U
U G J N R I I N V C I H S S
I N E A S N C K R R G C P C
T E F T G X C O T A C K W H
D C M D V I D R H S O C O R
E A A L H W A H I R M M G I
S Y N E H P E T S T N I A S
E G I R K A U E L Z M M C T
M S U A L C A T N A S A R E

Boxing Day	**Jesus Christ**	**Saint Stephen**
Christmas	**Partridge**	**Santa Claus**
England	**Pear**	**Wren**
Fruit		

CROSS STITCH DESIGN-HORUS

 hese are designs for cross stitch patterns that you can use for ornaments, throws or dishcloths. They are a work in progress, so if you can improve upon the design, go for it!!! The patterns might not all be up by Christmas Time, so if the pattern isn't up this week, check back again.

46

COLORING PAGES/RED WORK DESIGN-AUSTRALIAN SANTA WITH SIX WHITE BOOMERS

These are designs that can be used either for coloring pages for children or copied and transferred to cloth for Redwork for quilts. I kept the lines simple for both those reasons. Many of the designs have dots on them to sew miniature bells or gold beads on them to represent jingle bells.

Aussie Claus Australia

1 - Australia - Santa

Christmas in Australia is very hot. Whereas the northern hemisphere is in the middle of winter, Australians are baking in summer heat. It is not unusual to have Christmas Day well into the 90s! An Australian traditional meal includes a turkey dinner, with ham, and pork. A flaming Christmas plum pudding is added for dessert. In the Australian gold rushes, Christmas puddings often contained a gold nugget. Today a small favor is baked inside. Somewhat like the bean baked into the 12th Night cake. Whoever finds this knows s/he will enjoy good luck.

Many Australians prefer the image of huge Kangaroos pulling the sleigh across the sky instead of reindeer. This version has been made popular by an Australian Christmas carol sung by Rolf Harris "Six White Boomers" (boomers being slang for kangaroos, because of the boom sound they make as they land). It is also the title of a book of the same name about a baby Kangaroo called Joey, who becomes separated from his mother. Santa of course comes to the rescue, helping Joey find his mum with the aid of a sleigh pulled by Six White Boomers.

Some Australians and particularly tourists, often have their Christmas dinner at midday on a local beach. Other families enjoy their day by having a picnic. If they are at home, the day is punctuated by swimming in a pool, playing Cricket out the backyard, and other outdoor activities.

The warm weather allows Australians to enjoy a tradition which commenced in 1937. Carols by Candlelight is held every year on Christmas Eve, where tens of thousands of people gather in the city of Melbourne to sing their favorite Christmas songs. The evening is lit by as many candles singing under a clean cut night sky. The sky with its Southern Cross stars is like a mirror. Sydney and the other capital cities also enjoy Carols in the weeks leading up to Christmas. Australians surround themselves with Christmas Bush, a native plant which has little red flowered leaves.

At many beaches, Santa Claus arrives on a surfboard, boat or skidoos wearing board shorts and flip flops!!

50

TWO TURTLE DOVES

Since Ancient times, the dove has been associated with love and water. By the 1700's, turtledoves were a symbol of faithfulness and marital bliss.

Since Ancient times, the dove has been associated with love and water. By the 1700s, turtle doves were a symbol of faithfulness and marital bliss. Turtle doves are a common species of dove found in France and England. Back then, as today, doves were kept in cages as pets. Turtle doves also migrate to warmer climates in winter and their reappearance heralds the approach of spring. The turtle dove is a species that mates for life, so the giving of two turtle doves would have been a way an individual showed his/her eternal love for their intended.

Also known as Mother's Night and St. John's Day.

Mother's Night - Legends of beautiful Mother figures are associated with his day in Northern Europe.

St. John's Day - St. John, Apostle and Evangelist

This day is dedicated to the Disciple John. All the Church wine for the year would be blessed on this day in Germany and Austria. He is also the Patron Saint of Asia Minor. He became the "beloved disciple" that some theorize was actually Mary Magdalene, Jesus' wife. He wrote the fourth Gospel, and three Epistles, and the book of Revelation is also attributed to him.

BIBLICAL INTERPRETATION

The Two Turtle Doves symbolize the old and new testaments.

 he two Turtle Doves symbolize the Old and New Testaments.

54

ANOTHER CULTURE'S WINTER CELEBRATION

China - Dong Zhi

Winter solstice celebrations are also part of the cultural heritage of Pakistan and Tibet. December is known as the "Eleventh Moon". And in China, even though the calendar is based on the moon, the day of winter solstice is called Dong Zhi, "The Arrival of Winter." The cold of winter made an excellent excuse for a feast, so that's how the Chinese observed it, with Ju Dong, "doing the winter." Less than one percent of Chinese are Christian but those that are celebrate in somewhat the same way as people on this side of the pond. Their Shaman of goodies is called Dun Che Lao Ren, (pronounced Sheng dan lau ren) or Christmas Old Man. He is also known as "Lan Khoong-khoong" or "Nice Old Father".

He wears a long red robe, as red is a color of good luck. In China, as here, he brings presents for the good little boys and girls. They also have Christmas Trees, called Trees of Light. They decorate their homes with lights, paper lanterns, paper chains and flowers. It is a day for prayer and contemplation, family togetherness and good food.

In Japan, like China, not too many people are Christian. Those that are also celebrate Christmas, and their Santa is a round and jolly Monk named Hoteiosho. He wears a robe of red (of course) and carries a sack of goodies to those children who are deserving. He has very large earlobes, as he hears EVERYTHING about the little boys and girls he visits. In both countries, the Moon plays a major role in the festivals, with foods that are shaped like the full moon, scallops, dumplings and cookies; anything round and sweet.

Word Knerd

Waes Hael is an Old English term and it means Good Health or Be Well. It was used as a form of a salutation or greeting to which the reply would be, "Drink Hael". The phrase morphed into both a verb and a noun form (from Waes Hael to wassail) as people went "a-wassailing", going from house to house singing songs in exchange for food and drink. One of these drinks was, of course, wassail, a mixture of hot apple cider, spices, and frothy cream, called lambs wool.

Wassailing back in the day was a very complicated and detailed affair, with numerous events and ceremonies that HAD to take place in order for it to be successful. It began with a long procession to the orchards, where bowls of apple cider were poured amongst the apple tree roots, and bits of cider-soaked bread was placed in the tree's branches. Songs were sung and weapons were fired into the branches to scare away evil spirits and to bring luck to the New Year and the forthcoming harvest.

(See Caroles, Dances in the Round, Mummers)

Books

Dream Soul by Laurence Yep
ISBN 978-0-06-440788-5

The Legend of Papa Noel by
Teri Dunham
ISBN-9781585362561

58

 *Day 2*

REMEMBRANCES

 hese are the stories I collected from my friends, family, and people I met while traveling overseas, most notably from the Coalition Forces in Camp Bucca, Iraq. These stories are their most favorite memories of their Winter Celebrations and Traditions.

A Chinese Winter Solstice

Julie Yong | Compound 16, ECP Camp Bucca, Iraq

All throughout the year, I spent playing outside on the summer grass and kicking up fall leaves during recess at school. But, when winter came, there was one holiday I looked forward to, next to Christmas, that is. It was "Dong". It was a time to celebrate the changing of the autumn season to winter and to be at home with family, away from the cold shimmer of snowflakes to come.

Every year, my family would gather around the kitchen table after my mother would make "tong yuan", with my help of course. Winter melon, tiny bits of preserved shrimp, diced mushrooms, and radish—all had been chopped up uniformly. A rice flour mixture was rolled into marshmallow-y logs first, then half dollar sized bits were formed into little snowballs and tossed into the wok one by one to make a soupy sea of vegetables and crustaceans more mouthwatering. A dish like this would warm anyone up, and it especially made a family gathering more enjoyable—when all my relatives praised her cooking and expertise in the kitchen. Slicing and dicing the ingredients and adding just the right amount of pepper and salt (without the use of measuring utensils) was a skill no one in the family had ever contested.

Now the great thing after every holiday meal at my home was bonding in front of the TV, and setting oneself comfortably on the couch to fall asleep. My nine year old frame shrunk into the fetal position, as all chatter about how great the meal was, or plans for another family get together were fading into the distant background. By the time I wake up and make my way upstairs to bed, the dishes are done, the TV off, and my parents are reading the paper, while all the rest of my relatives are long gone.

A Memory of Dong Zhi

Sam Wu | Cary, North Carolina

Dong Zhi is the Winter Solstice. As with any Holiday, it should be festive and enjoyable. This was NOT the case with my first Winter Solstice. Moving is a hectic thing, what with the packing and unpacking of more than thirty boxes, not a fun or easy task. Therefore, as Dong Zhi rolled around, our apartment was still occupied by cardboard boxes and baggage trunks, taped and untouched since the middle of August when we arrived in China. Our winter attire, the jackets, sweaters and scarves that were so necessary in the wet, cold, gray Shanghai winters, were still in their boxes. My mother, seeing that it was already "mid-winter," decided that unpacking could no longer be put off. The morn-

ing passed in a chaotic blur of activity. Heavy luggage boxes were lugged into bedrooms only to be discovered full of plates and cutlery. Half the contents of a trunk were sorted into my closet before I realized that the pink sweater and bunny mittens meant the clothes were all my sisters.

Finally, at half-past seven, well past the time we were due at my grandparents, we left our opened boxes scattered throughout the apartment. After dinner at Grandpa's (which was mercifully better than my mom's cooking that I had expected as our dinner) Grandpa said, "Well, since you are all done, come and help us down, unpack, and clean the stuff we have in storage. You won't mind since today's a holiday and you've had a day to play, right?

Another story:

Sam Wu | Cary, North Carolina

January (or into late February to early March by the traditional calendar) is a good month. First (and foremost to any student), it has a week-long vacation to accommodate the two very important holidays. Chinese New Year and Yuan Dan. Secondly, to the chagrin of the adults and the delight of the children, quite a bit of money is given out in red envelopes. 3,000 Yen or about 375 dollars isn't bad for a day or two's work of bowing and wishing a felicitous New Year to relatives. Lastly, the food is glorious!!!

For a week or two before New Year's Eve, all time and resources are devoted to the preparation of food: giant prawns, fried and served in a somewhat sweet and salty sauce; a large fish, battered and fried, and covered in every conceivable brightly colored ornamentation and served with a creamy tomato sauce; the hearts of Bok Choy arranged in rings; thin slices of beef, fried and drowned in spices; and of course, there is potluck. All known foods and quite a few unknowns go into the pot-luck. So plentiful are the dishes that the table to accommodate them takes up the entire living room of my grandparents' admittedly tiny apartment. If you sit down, you are obliged to continue until everyone is done, since there is nowhere to excuse yourself to. Following the feast, when everyone is too full to move, the TV is turned on. Those who designed the annual TV show that encompasses everything from singing to torch juggling atop five men on one unicycle are shrewd enough to realize that TV is the only viable "activity" after such a meal. Towards midnight, as the show draws to an end, firecrackers and fireworks are set off. It is widely known that New Year's Eve is the busiest time for Firefighters, as they are constantly summoned to deal with those who have set fire to their neighbor's laundry or worse yet, the irate neighbors themselves, who stuck their heads out the window to yell at the offenders.

By comparison, Yuan Dan is a much tamer holiday, though it also involves gorging. In place of TV shows and firecrackers are the wheeled lanterns. The pastime for kids is to drag a lantern (often rabbit-shaped) around. More often than not, this "Festival of Lights" turns into a race, complete with the inevitable crushed lanterns and bruised and crying children.

All in all, the holidays, along with their mishaps, are still enjoyable as they are important to the culture of China. After all, who can deny the importance of money?

RECIPES

 ere, I add recipes for the day: both traditional and from a different country/culture. I hope that you will try a few of these recipes and perhaps incorporate them into your family traditions.

Tang Yuan

I worked for a wonderful organization called Prison Fellowship for a while when I first moved to North Carolina, (Hi Ed...hi Rose!) and one week, we had an intern named Sam who was Chinese and whose mom still cooked (badly as Sam reported but with enthusiasm) traditional Chinese dishes. He contributed two of the Remembrance Stories below and he also told me of an interesting dish served at Winter Solstice called Tang Yuan and sweet dumplings with sugar no less. Filled dumplings with sweet syrup over them. Sigh. ok, anyways. I tried the recipe his mom gave me and it was very good. Of course, as you try recipes out so you can write about them, you find out what tastes good and what doesn't. What works for you and what doesn't. (Translation: what you screwed up and what worked by a miracle of God ☺)

This recipe called for making a syrup out of Chinese log sugar. First it was hard to find it and second, when I DID find it apparently it is a VERY bad idea to add cold butter to hot boiling sugar syrup on the stove. I won't go into details but suffice it to say . . . that part of the recipe you are on your own with. We will just say "Ouch" with emphasis and leave it at that.

I reverted to my Vermonty roots and boiled MY Tang Yuan in maple syrup. That's the second best part of this recipe. Nothing smells as good as Vermont maple syrup on the boil. I am standing there, boiling away, stirring the little green and red balls of rice dough around in my yummy syrup, waiting for them to rise to the top, when it occurs to me I am making glue. It really was one of those Eureka moments. Glue. I am getting excited here, smelling yummy things and I am really just making glue. Dumplings are primarily water and flour. Paste is water and flour. The critical difference between the two is the amount used of either ingredient and the use of flavoring. But it all boils down (haha) to proper chemistry, which I failed in High School, so use Sam's recipe to the letter, buy pre-made syrup and make sure you wear long sleeves when you boil the dumplings. Seriously.

Ingredients

- 1 cup glutinous rice flour

- Water (told you....it's glue)

- Food coloring

- ¼ cup ground up Red Hots

- ½ cup coconut flakes

Directions

When you make these dumplings, Sam told me his mother would color them green and red with food coloring. He also said you could add other flavorings for different tastes. So I used ground up Red Hots for the red dumplings, coconut for the white ones and left the green ones plain. Traditional Tang Yuan can have fillings of ground red bean paste or other Chinese sweets but I honestly didn't have the courage to venture further into that particular direction.

In a bowl, add the rice flour. Then add the water tablespoon by tablespoon until it gets to a dough-like consistency. Divide into three portions. In one portion, add a few drops of red food coloring and 1/4 cup of the finely ground Red Hots (I used a coffee grinder at the store). Mix well and then pinch off small bits and roll into a ball the size of a marble (No bigger, then it gets too doughy!).

Take the second ball of dough and mix well with the half cup of coconut. Make the dumplings marble sized as well.

Take the third and add a few drops of green food coloring. I used red and green as they are the Traditional Yule colors and Red are the color of Good Luck in China at this time of year.

Heat a saucepan with water. Put the syrup in another saucepan on low or medium heat. When the water comes to a boil, drop in a few of the colored glue balls, um, dumplings and wait. When the dumplings rise to the top, use a slotted spoon and transfer them to a bowl to cool. After a few minutes, place them in the hot syrup. When they rise to the top again, they are done. Serve immediately in small bowls with a small amount of the syrup poured over the top.

Tong Yuan

Ingredients

- 2 handfuls of dried mushrooms

- 1 small bag of rice flour

- 1 medium-sized Winter Melon

- 1 handful of dried shrimp

- 1 medium-sized radish

Directions

Soak dried shrimp for 25 minutes and also soak mushrooms until softened, then dice into 1/4" thick slices, peel winter melon and radish, gut out seeds, slice into 1/4 -1/2" slices 1 1/2" lengthwise. Mix rice flour, a pinch of salt and enough water into a thick paste and set aside.

When cooking, place winter melon and radish with a cup of water in a wok and let boil. Then add mushrooms, shrimp and more water. Then take the flour mixture and roll it into logs, pinch off half dollar size pieces and roll into balls, drop into the wok one at a time. After the last piece is in, cook for another 20-25 minutes, then serve.

Caramel Dumplings

These are my Aunt Nancy's dessert dumplings, and again, there really isn't anything bad you can say against dumplings and caramel. I tried one and fell in love, but then brought the rest to work. I love trying recipes but I know when I am in trouble!! Or rather, I know when my butt is in trouble!

Ingredients

Sauce:

- 2 tbsp. butter

- 1 ½ cup packed brown sugar

- 1 ½ cups water

- 1/8 tsp. salt

Dumplings:

- 1¼ cup flour

- 1 tbsp. butter

- 1/3 cup sugar

- ½ cup milk

- 1/8 tsp. salt

- ½ tsp. vanilla

- ½ tsp. baking powder

Directions

Place ingredients for the sauce in a large saucepan. Simmer while preparing the dough. Mix together in a small bowl the flour, sugar, salt and baking powder. A teaspoon of cinnamon can be added (Go ahead, I did and it was great!!) Blend in the butter, milk and vanilla. Mix well.

Drop large spoonfuls of the mixture into the sauce. Cover the pan and do not remove the lid for 20 minutes. Serve warm with Cool Whip.

Chicken and Dumplings

This is a quick and easy recipe for chicken and dumplings; you can increase the size of the portions by adding more chicken breasts and using another can of soup.

Ingredients

- 2 chicken breasts, cubed

- 1 medium-sized onion, diced

- 2 tbsp. butter

- 1 small can of peas (yuck!) or corn or cooked carrots

- 1 can Cream of Chicken soup (when increasing the amounts, use a can of Cream of Mushroom to add flavor)

Dumplings:

- 2 eggs, beaten
- ½ cup all purpose flour
- ¾ stick butter softened
- ½ tsp. salt

Directions

In a bowl, mix the flour and the eggs. Into this mixture, add the softened butter and the salt. Mix well. Roll out on a floured surface and cut out small circles of dough using the open end of a water glass, about three inches wide.

Preheat the oven to 400°F.

In a deep saucepan, sauté the onions with two tablespoons of butter. Add the chicken and cook slightly. Add the Cream of Chicken soup and your vegetable of choice. Cook for a few minutes. Pour contents into a 9x13 baking dish. Cover with the round circles of dough, covering the chicken mixture. Bake for 25 minutes or until dumplings are slightly brown.

70

Day 2

PUZZLES

```
F T E S T A M E N T S A E N
A D O N G Z H I Q Y I D M M
I R M O T H E R S N I G H T
T A M E T C C E L C F T R X
H T U R T L E D O V E S Y P
F O R U W C C C I O A C P A
U N O O M H T N E V E L E Y
L G E B Y I Y P I J W G P O
N X K S G N I L P M U D V B
E I D W D A L L O V E E R X
S B F W F Z J C L S E O N I
S M A R I T A L B L I S S N
```

China	Faithfulness	Mother's night
Dong Zhi	Love	Testaments
Dumplings	Marital Bliss	Turtle Doves
Eleventh Moon		

Day 2

CROSS STITCH DESIGN - CHRISTIAN FISH

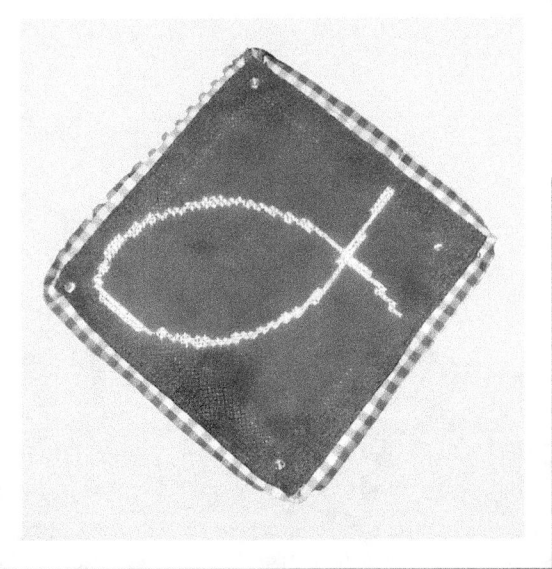

These are designs for cross stitch patterns that you can use for ornaments, throws or dishcloths. They are a work in progress, so if you can improve upon the design, go for it!!! The patterns might not all be up by Christmas time, so if the pattern isn't up this week, check back again.

74

COLORING PAGES/RED WORK DESIGN - DUN RE LAO CHEN/CHRISTMAS OLD MAN – CHINESE SANTA AND HOTEIOSHO - JAPANESE SANTA

hese are designs that can be used either for coloring pages for children or copied and transferred to cloth for Redwork for quilts. I kept the lines simple for both those reasons. Many of the designs have dots on them to show where to sew miniature bells or gold beads on them to represent jingle bells.

Christmas Old Man

圣诞老人

Dun Che
Lao Ren
China

Hotelosho
Japan

2 - China - Dun Che Lao Ren

Less than one percent of the Chinese population are Christians. Those that are, however, celebrate Christmas. The Christian children of China decorate trees with colorful ornaments. These ornaments are made from paper in the shapes of flowers, chains and lanterns. The Chinese Christmas trees are called Trees of Light and Santa Claus is called Dun Che Lao Ren which means "Christmas Old Man."

Like children in America, Chinese children also hang stockings hoping that Christmas Old Man will fill them with gifts and treats. Parents and grandparents give out gifts of money in red envelopes, which are a symbol of good luck. A favorite dish to eat is called Tang Yuan, sweet rice flour dumplings in syrup.

Another name for this season is "The Spring Festival" and many families celebrate with festivities that include delicious meals and pay respects to their ancestors. In these celebrations, children are the main focus, they receive new clothes and toys, eat delectable food and watch firecracker displays.

5 - Japan - Hoteiosho

In Japan, less than one percent of Japanese are Christians, so the Christmas holiday has only been observed for about the last one hundred years. The observance of the Holiday is mainly commercial and closely tied to the American urban Christmas. Carols are sung in Japanese, Christmas trees are decorated with lights, turkeys are fattened, and mistletoe and holly are hung.

Young adults in Japan treat this Holiday as a romantic holiday. Couples buy cards and flowers, go to parties and dress in red, which is considered a very lucky color. A Christmas Cake is the most popular confection sold, a white cake decorated with Strawberries. Most bakeries are often sold out days in advance of Christmas and to buy a Christmas cake after Christmas is considered very unlucky.

Instead of adopting the American Santa Claus, the Japanese looked into their own tradition to find someone with similar characteristics. This was Hoteiosho, a Buddhist monk/old Japanese god. He was originally one of the seven gods of good fortune. An amiable, serene and contented deity, he is often represented as a Buddhist priest with large earlobes, which are said to hear everything the children say—their version of "He knows when you are sleeping, he knows when you're awake, he knows when you are bad or good . . ." He is always shown laughing and smiling. He carries a fan or a walking stick in one hand and his bag of "Precious Things" in the other. His belly is huge and is said to be a symbol of the size of his soul. His robes drape around his big belly and are a lucky color red.

Day 3

HISTORICAL INTERPRETATION

> Three French hens may be a play on words, as France used to be known as Gaul, which in Latin is gaillie which is similar to the roman word for rooster. White hens are also considered a symbol of motherhood and good luck.

Three French Hens may be a play on words, as France used to be called Gaul, which sounds similar to the Roman word for Rooster, Gallie. Which also sounds similar to the Latin word for France which is Gaillie. White hens, and like many white animals, are a symbol of good luck.

Also known as Boy Bishop Day.

Boy Bishop Day - Another example of the holdover of traditions from the even "older" times, the Feast of Fools and Saturnalia. This is another example of role reversal in strict societies of the day; a boy would be elected Bishop and allowed to preside over church activities and celebrations on this day.

BIBLICAL INTERPRETATION

The Three French Hens symbolize the Christian virtues of Faith, Hope and Charity.

Three French Hens are a symbol of the three Virtues of the Christian Faith: Faith, Hope and Charity

82

ANOTHER CULTURE'S WINTER CELEBRATION

Shab-e Yalda - Iran

In Iran, there is the observance of Shab-e Yalda, in which families keep vigil through the night and fires burn brightly to help the sun (and Goodness) battle darkness (thought evil). Yalda has a history as long as the Mithraism religion. The Mithraists believed that this night is the night of the birth of Mithra, Persian god of light and truth. On the morning of the longest night of the year Mithra, the Sun God, is born from a virgin mother.

Yalda became a social occasion when family and close friends would get together. They would all come together and sit at the Korsi, a small, short square table. The tradition was to stay awake all night so as to properly greet the new day with fresh fruit left over from the harvest. Most often, watermelons and pomegranates are eaten. They have a special reverence for the colors of peach, yellows, soft reds and pinks, the colors of the sunrise, a celebration of the sun. This eating of fruits during the winter is to symbolize the ancient customs of invoking the divinities to request protection of the winter crop.

The 13th century Persian poet Sa'di wrote in his Bustan: "The true morning will not come, until the Yalda Night is gone".

The Eve of the Yalda has great significance in the Persian/Iranian calendar, as it is the eve of the birth of Mithra, the Sun God, who symbolized light, goodness and strength on earth.

REMEMBRANCES

 hese are the stories I collected from my friends, family and people I met while traveling overseas, most notably from the Coalition Forces in Camp Bucca, Iraq. These stories are their most favorite memories of their Winter Celebrations and Traditions.

A Christmas Tradition

by someone Who Doesn't Much Care For Christmas
Katy R. (my LITTLE sister!!)
Alexandria, Virginia

The sad but honest truth is that I'm not a big fan of Christmas. Sure, I could offer up the usual complaints about how the Christmas holiday is over-commercialized, stressful, and has lost its real meaning. But the real problem is I forgot about what Christmas was like when I was a child. So for far too long I dismissed Christmas with a "Bah-Humbug!" and cited a busy work schedule as my reason for glossing over the season. I attended the occasional holiday party and dutifully carried out last minute shopping for gifts, but I hardly reveled in the Season. On the contrary, I generally tried to slip unnoticed past Christmas until the mall decorations came down and the coast was clear.

That is, until I met my husband. He loves Christmas. I mean, he *really loves* Christmas—and embraces it with a wonderful sense of joy and spirit. And once it became clear how fired up he was about the holidays, I realized I would have to actually take action, or it would get out of control. Because as it turns out, we have rather different ideas of Christmas decorations. I'll be blunt in saying that enveloping our house with a thousand blinking lights and stationing cheerful snowmen and smiling Santas at the front door was a little alien to me.

I remember my parents carefully unpacking delicate little wooden and glass ornaments they'd bought in Germany, and after we kids had strung our garlands of cranberries and popcorn on the tree, we'd spend the entire evening decorating it with the ornaments. Each one was so unique, and I always especially loved the wooden figures of chimney sweeps and ladies with their rosy cheeks and detailed garments. Each little person took their place on the tree, and after the New Year we wrapped them carefully with tissue paper and back in the box they went.

With that memory in mind, I resurrected my Christmas spirit and took a small stand against my husband's decorating ambitions. The battle lines were drawn—he could do whatever he wished with the outside of the house, but the tree was mine. Only one problem remained—I didn't actually own any little wooden ornaments. Luckily, we were stationed in Europe, as my parents had been years ago, and my husband took me to the German Christmas markets in search of ornaments. We trudged through dozens of vendor's stalls, only finding nicely crafted wooden pieces here, because most on offer now says "Made in China" and didn't look at all as I remembered.

Saint that he is, my husband missed out on some great beer and fireside chats at the pub to take me on this mission. But we journeyed home with a treasure trove of new ornaments and decorated the tree with simple white lights, small wooden apples, and the traditional German ornaments. It looked just like I remembered. No pink glittery ornaments, peacock feathers, or cutesy kittens hanging from the branches. After that first Christmas together we resolved to look for handcrafted ornaments whenever we travel, and now it has become our tradition to decorate the tree with unique glass and wooden pieces from around the globe.

Hotel for Dogs or Room at the Inn

Heather M.
San Antonio, Texas
(My BIG sister!)

My favorite Holiday memories started about two years ago. Adam and I found two pit bulls mixed breed puppies and took them in. Frieda (our mutt) loved them so much and we had a blast with them until their owners claimed them. It gave us the idea to get our own pit bull mix puppy, Coco. Then this last Christmas, some idiot decided to dump a little blonde Yorkie puppy wrapped up in a towel up against our neighbor's garage. We felt so bad for the little guy, we took him in too and he stayed with us for almost two months before we found him a home.

We had named him Buddy, and it was really hard to let him go. He is in a good home now and doing great. We also buy toys for SAM's Shelter every Christmas and I do it wearing my Santa's Hat!! Every Thanksgiving and Christmas usually finds us with a stray or two in addition to our own two dogs, two dogs and an albino Ferret named Lucky. I guess the moral of the story is that there is always room at the inn.

Day 3

RECIPES

 ere, I add recipes for the day: both traditional and from a different country/culture. I hope that you will try a few of these recipes and perhaps incorporate them into your family traditions.

Baked Chicken

I blew up a chicken once. I totally didn't mean to, but I did. In front of my dinner guest too. Who was a man. Not a date sort of man, not a romantical situation; just a buddy-pal-friend-o'-mine-can-I-sleep-on-your-couch kinda friend. It was only Jesse, one of the guys from my Unit, but still. It was humiliating. He still teases me about that, although he wasn't saying too much when I ordered an emergency backup pizza.

That's when I learned the difference between Pyrex made of lime soda and Pyrex made of borosilicate glass. Way back in the day, there used to be a company named Corning (as in Corningware). They made Pyrex dishes. The material they used was called borosilicate glass that wouldn't shatter even with a great temperature difference. NOW, all Corning Pyrex is made with soda lime glass and is NOT even close to being as resilient as the older stuff made of borosilicate glass. Even opening the oven door will cause it to implode with the introduction of cooler air. Look for the OLD Pyrex on eBay. It is worth its weight in gold.

I actually saw an episode about exploding chickens (and other meats) on Mythbusters about a year after my Chicken Incident. God Bless Mythbusters and their insane sideways thinking. Exploding Chickens. You can't make that stuff up! So make sure you DO NOT baste or place liquids in the pan in which you are baking said chicken. DO NOT place the baking dish on a marble or granite countertop in a relatively cool kitchen. In fact, don't even use glass. Use a metal one. I am still traumatized.

Anyways, my cousin's ex gave me a foolproof (shut up, Dad!) recipe for baked chicken. I tried it with a METAL PAN and it was fabulous. Really. It is probably the simplest recipe you will ever use and the leftovers will make you smile. If there are leftovers.

Ingredients

- 1 small roasting chicken, about 5 lbs. Perdue is good. It has that thermometer already in it.

- ½ unsalted butter sliced into small pieces

- 2 cups chicken stock

- 1 packet onion soup mix

- 1 large onion, quartered

- 6 carrots, peeled and sliced

- 8 medium-sized potatoes, peeled and chopped into small chunks

- salt and pepper

Directions

Preheat the oven to 400°F.

Take the chicken out of the package and rinse it well under cool water. Make sure there is no giblet package inside, you don't want any unpleasant surprises AFTER you've finished cooking it!! Rinse inside and outside of the bird. Then, using your bare fingers (feels really icky but your hands are so smooth afterward) separate the skin from the carcass, but don't pull it off. Slip the sliced butter pieces in between the meat and the skin in various locations all over the chicken. DO NOT butter the outside of the chicken. Salt and pepper to taste.

Place the cut up veggies of your choice into a METAL roasting pan. Mix the two cups of chicken stock with the packet of onion soup mix and pour over the vegetables. Take the chicken and place it on top of the vegetables, taking care to make sure the wings and legs are not touching the sides of the pan. You might want to take some cooking twine, tie the legs up, and tuck the wings underneath the body while roasting. You can put some of the veggies in the cavity of the bird.

Bake for 20 minutes per pound. The temperature gauge should pop up when the bird is done but a good rule of thumb is that the chicken should be at 185 F before you eat it. Take the pan out of the oven and place on the stovetop to let it settle.

Watermelon Pie

The people who celebrate Shab-e Yalda favor the pink, red, and orange fruits for desserts at this festival in honor of the sun and its rising on the new day. I was going to use a peach cobbler recipe but anyone can make a peach cobbler. So I looked for and found a Watermelon Pie recipe. Yup. A watermelon pie. The first one actually has sesame seeds, and flour base for the crust and a complicated

mixture in between. Haven't tried that one yet. But I did find a nice one that uses Jello mix. It is a very simple recipe, not overly sweet and really good. I used kiwi slices on top to contrast the gentle pink color.

Ingredients

For the crust:

*   Use a pre-made graham cracker crust OR 1 1/4 cup of graham cracker crumbs

*   1/3 stick melted butter

*   ¼ cup sugar

For the filling:

*   1 cup heavy cream

*   1 kiwi, sliced

*   1/2 cup milk

*   1 tablespoon lemon juice

*   ½ cup watermelon juice, fully blended to a liquid with no juice

*   ½ cup sugar

*   2 tsp. Watermelon flavored jello mix

Directions

Preheat the oven to 400°F. Mix ingredients for crust in a small bowl until thoroughly mixed. Press into the bottom of a nine-inch greased pie pan, glass is best. Bake for 15 minutes or until the edges are slightly brown. Remove and let cool completely before filling.

PUZZLES

```
P U N P U O I P E P E T C Z V
I U E O J Q E G I P D U O M Z
W A T E R M E L O N A R I U V
M U T D M S F R E T S O O R J
S E H U T U N G O O D L U C K
H V O W P O M E G R A N A T E
T O P O E G Y D H U H S O E D
X P E E Y E O I C H T T O I E
A D L A Y E B A H S C G I X M
W H I T E H E N S I A N A A K
D O O H R E H T O M P R E U F
F U B E B P U C B U I S D R L
A S O O B Y C H A R I T Y U F
```

Charity	Hope	Rooster
Faith	Iran	Shab e Yalda
French Hens	Motherhood	Watermelon
Gaul	Pomegranate	White Hens
Good Luck		

COLORING PAGES/RED WORK DESIGN - CAJUN SANTA - BAYOU BOAT PULLED BY EIGHT ALLIGATORS

hese are designs that can be used either for coloring pages for children or copied and transferred to cloth for Redwork for quilts. I kept the lines simple for both those reasons. Many of the designs have dots on them to show where to sew miniature bells or gold beads on them to represent jingle bells.

Cajun Santa
Deep South

Word Knerd

This history of the word Monday

Latin	Germanic/Norse Gods	Spanish	English
Dies Lunes	Montag or Moon Day	Lunes	Monday
Day of Moon			

Books

Night of The Moon
By Hena Khan
ISBN-9780811860628

98

BUILDING TWELVE DAYS OF CHRISTMAS BLOCKS

Y ou might have noticed the carved wooden blocks on each page for the 12 Days of Christmas. These are wooden blocks with each of the six sides covered with a history of the verse, a visual of another Culture's Winter Celebration, the number of the day and yet another name the day is known by. I wanted to sell these, but it has proven thus far to be an expensive proposition. So I went and made an aluminum set, made of recycled aluminum. While visually stunning, and a nice mantelpiece display, it also proved too pricey to mass produce on my budget.

Soooo, I decided on two alternative methods that are cost effective AND appeal to the Uber Moms out there. There are instructions to make both paper blocks and cloth blocks with color transfer copies on them. Below find the instructions to put together your own set of the Twelve Days of Christmas Culture Blocks.

Paper Blocks:

1. Print out the template for the paper box; enlarge the template by exactly 172%, it will fit precisely onto an 18x24 paper for 3" blocks.

2. Print out the line drawings for a particular day you wish to create.

3. Color in the drawings.

4. Cut out and paste into squares.

5. Cut out and assemble paper blocks using tacky glue on the side tabs.

6. Let dry for one hour and enjoy!!!

Blocks Template:

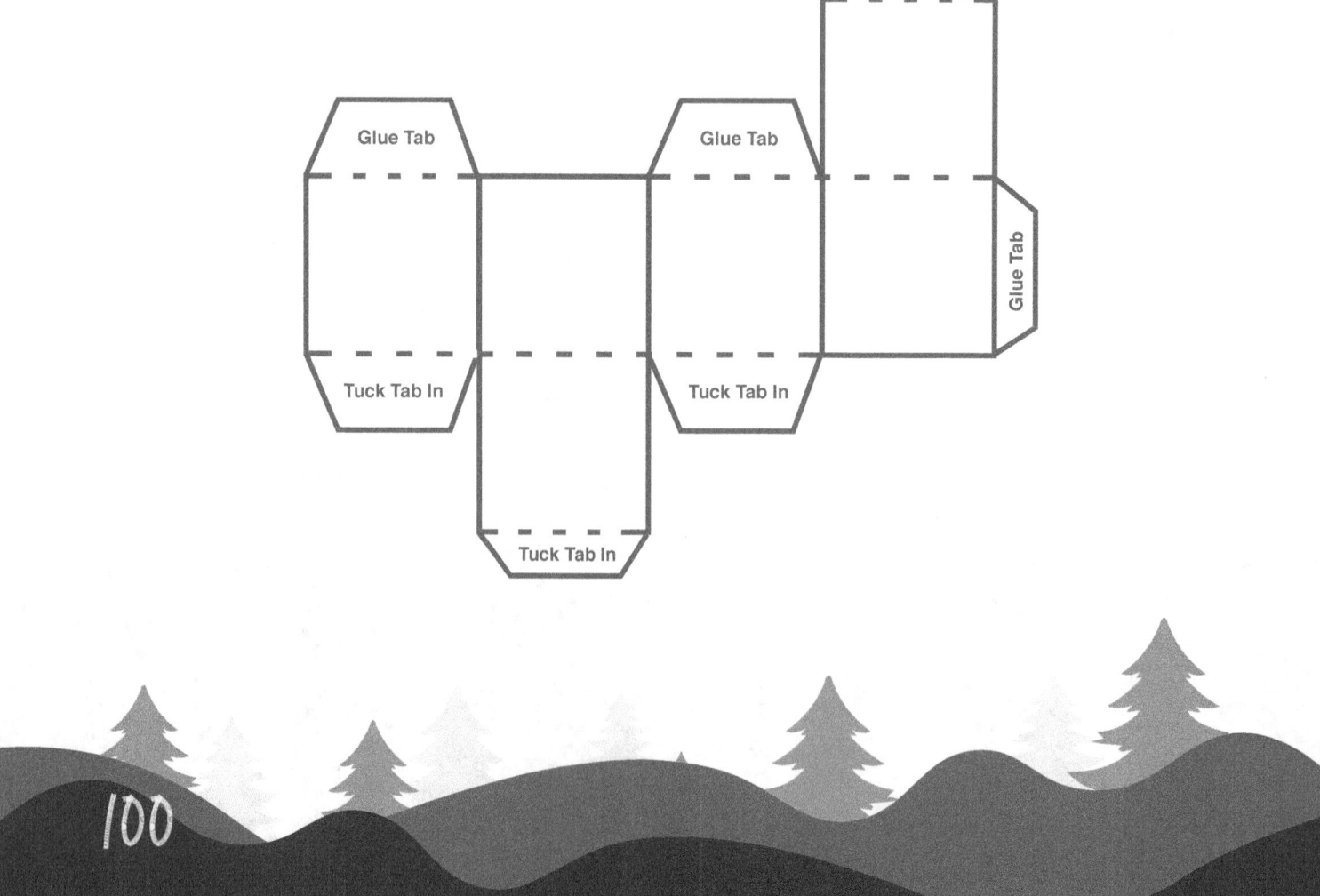

Box Pictures:

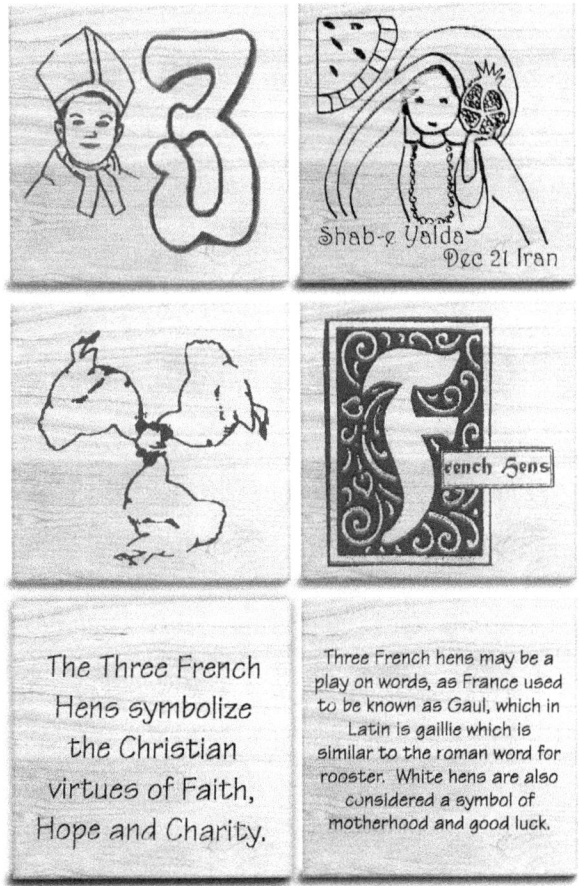

Cloth Blocks:

1. Buy a yard and a half of plain white muslin.

2. Cut out 72 pieces of three-and-a-half-inch squares of fabric and set aside.

3. Cut out one dozen 3x3" squares out of cardstock. I used old greeting cards and they worked great!

4. Print out the line drawings for a particular day you wish to create.

5. Color in the drawings.

6. Using Color Copy Transfer paper (available at JoAnn's, Micheals and A.C. Moore) print the colored in drawings out.

7. Iron on the six designs, one each onto six pieces of three and a half squares of muslin.

To assemble each box:

1. Lay a muslin square over each square of cardstock and firmly baste onto the square using a running stitch

2. Laying right sides together, use a white thread OR (just to be different) a brightly colored floss, two strands, to stitch the fabric at the top of the two cards together.

3. Sew together four in a row before joining two end to end to create the base for the box, right sides facing out

4. Carefully stitch the 5th square to the open end of the box

5. Stitch the 6th and final square onto the open end, leaving one seam open to remove the card stock.

Now you have a choice. You can either leave the card stock in and sew it up tight to end up with a stable and firm box, OR... you can snip the basting stitches and remove the cardboard, stuff the blocks with batting and sew up the final seam, to have soft, squeezable blocks. This is what I did with my example blocks and they look GREAT sitting in a basket by the fireplace. Plus, they are plush and soft and kids love to handle them. If you leave the cardboard shapes in, they will retain their nice square edges but you have to be careful of getting them wet and they will get sort of squidgy around the edges over time.

COLORING PAGES/RED WORK DESIGN - CAJUN SANTA - BAYOU BOAT PULLED BY EIGHT ALLIGATORS

These are designs that can be used either for coloring pages for children or copied and transferred to cloth for Rework for quilts. I kept the lines simple for both of those reasons. Many of the designs have dots on them to show where to sew miniature bells or gold beads on them to represent jingle bells. If you would like to buy all fourteen designs for only 10 dollars, please go to the store and use Paypal and download the designs.

Bayou Santa

9 - United States - Bayou Santa / Papa Noel

Papa Noel or the Cajun Santa Claus is the Southern American version of Santa. He wears a fur suit in some versions and in others, a pair of bib overalls. In all versions his mode of transportation, whatever it may be (a swamp boat, a pirogue, which is a Cajun canoe, a skiff) is pulled by eight or nine alligators. The lead alligator, the alternate "Rudolph," is most often white with a green eye, which would be a Southern nod to the American tradition of having albino animals being sacred or animals endowed with special powers. Cajun Claus speaks in the Cajun patois, half French and half English and in all the versions he mentions local names, songs and of course, food.

FOUR COLLY BIRDS

Colly means black as colly is derived from the word coal. Colly birds means blackbirds and blackbird pie was a delicacy in medieval times.

elieve it or not, it is NOT "The Four Calling Birds" although that does make sense. It is actually a bastardized form of the word Coal. Colly is slang for "coal" which means black. Colly birds means Blackbirds and blackbird pie was a delicacy in Medieval times. Most anything and everything that could be cooked were baked into a pie.

Also known as Saturnalia and Feast of Fools

108

BIBLICAL INTERPRETATION

The Four Colly Birds symbolize the four gospels of Matthew, Mark Luke and John.

The Four Colly Birds symbolize the four Gospels of Matthew, Mark, Luke, and John.

110

ANOTHER CULTURE'S WINTER CELEBRATION

Saturnalia - Rome
Yo Saturnalia!!!!!

Ok, it's actually written Io Saturnalia… but it's pronounced Yo!!! Don't you just love how YO! is actually a come back phrase? LOL! And back in the day, Roman days, that was the customary greeting on this week-long festival in honor of the God Saturn, God of the Harvest/Seeds.

The 13th-century Persian poet Sa'di wrote in his Bustan: "The true morning will not come, until the Yalda Night is gone".

The Eve of the Yalda has great significance in the Persian/Iranian calendar. It is the eve of the birth of Mithra, the Sun God, who symbolized light, goodness, and strength on earth.

Now, if you think modern-day culture has commercialized Christmas past what is good and proper, you are not alone in your beliefs. In fact, you are several thousand years behind some of the first lamenters of the "destruction of a holy day by drink and mirth". The early Romans knew excess when they saw it and of course there were Elders who disapproved of the goings on of the City. Just like there were those who disapproved of the fairs and games and partying in the 1600s, when Cromwell brought the hammer down on celebrating Christmas. People were actually fined if they closed their shops on Christmas day.

The disapproval about the way the celebrations were carried out started back in Roman Times about Saturnalia and went through the Christian world from the 1600s in England to the 1800s in the Americas. Below, you will find a few of the quotes from the Ancients and the Old Ones about how the young'uns keep screwing up the Holidays and how commercialization of a sacred event will be the downfall of us all. The way I look at it, "they" have been complaining about it for over 2000 plus years and "we" still find ways to honor the events. I doubt the "real" reason behind the season will ever be lost.

Read below:

> It is now the month of December, when the greatest part of the city is in a bustle. Loose reins are given to public dissipation; everywhere you may hear the sound of great preparations, as if there were some real difference between the days devoted to Saturn and those for transacting business.... Were you here, I would willingly confer with you as to the plan of our conduct; whether we should eve in our usual way, or, to avoid singularity, both take a better supper and throw off the toga.
>
> Seneca the younger-- From the Epistolae around 50 A.D

> "Rich or poor, whoever he is, he boasts that he shares the table of the emperor."
>
> ---Statius, writing of the Feast of Saturn (1st century AD).

> During My week the serious is barred; no business allowed. Drinking, noise and games and dice, appointing of kings and feasting of slaves, singing naked, clapping of frenzied hands, an occasional ducking of corked faces in icy water—such are the functions over which I preside.
>
> ---Lucian, Saturnalia

Continue on page 113 >>

from page 112 >>

It was celebrated in ancient times by the rustic population as a sort of joyous harvest-home, and in every age was viewed by all classes of the community as a period of absolute relaxation and unrestrained merriment. During its continuance no public business could be transacted, the law courts were closed, the schools kept holiday, to commence a war was impious, to punish a malefactor involved pollution.

--- Macrobius

"When Saturn rules, all things are turned around, and everything becomes its opposite."

Saturnalia was a time of revelry and fun. Saturnus, the God of Seed and Sowing, was honored with a Festival from December 17th to December 23rd. During this holiday, normal restrictions were relaxed. Gambling was allowed in public, men dressed as women and women dressed as men. Masters would serve their servants and vice versa. Gifts were given, little terra cotta or wax doll figures.

In Ancient, ancient times, there used to be human sacrifices in attempts to lure the sun back to the sky, but as time went on and human life became more precious, doll figures were substituted. Traditionally, silver was "the" gift to give for the upper classes, although the lower classes usually gave dolls, drink and food. Quarrels were forgotten, or at least put aside for the week, and merriment reigned!! This also is a lead in for the other huge party of the Season, the Feast of Fools. It was during this time of role reversal that huge banquets were held.

A Lord of Misrule was elected to preside over the festivities. Most of the banquets were costume balls or masquerades, which aided in the whole men dressing as women and vice versa. Yet another time of "too much is too much!!" came about in the 1660s when the Church of England decided that the Birth of Christ was no reason to party and tried to clamp down on the Winter Celebrations. Look up Church Reformation and Cromwell for more details.

Word Knerd

This history of the word Tuesday

Latin	Germanic/Norse Gods	Spanish	English
Dies Martis	Mars or Tyw	Martes	Tuesday
Day of Mars			

Books

The Shortest Day:
Celebrating the Winter Solstice by Wendy Pfeffer
ISBN-9780525469681

Day 4

REMEMBRANCES

olly Birds

hese are the stories I collected from my friends, family and people I met while traveling overseas, most notably from the Coalition Forces in Camp Bucca, Iraq. These stories are their most favorite memories of their Winter Celebrations and Traditions.

A New England Christmas

Paul Shepard
Lunenburg, Vermont

The earliest Christmases I remember go back to the early 1950s, when I would have been eight or ten years old. Our family celebrated Christmas at home, but we also went to my grandmothers for the big Christmas at the old farmhouse at the top of Sanborn Hill. Grammy had eight children and most of them would show up with their spouse and their children, so there would be twenty-five or more people there. The old farmhouse would be big enough for everyone there, even though it had no electricity, no running water, no plumbing and no insulation.

Everyone drew names for next year, so everyone only got one gift, but somehow Grammy always managed to knit each grandchild a pair of wool socks or mittens. The highlight of the day, for the kids anyway, was the smell of homemade bread, apple pies, pumpkin pies, turkey and all the rest of it, cooking over a wood stove and somehow all getting hot and ready at the same time.

Normally, the old farmhouse was cold and drafty but on Christmas with so many people and all that cooking it was warm and cheery and smelled great!!!

Santa's Milk and Cookies

David H. (my DAD!!)
Windsor, Vermont

When I was a kid, my sister Nancy and I really got into the Christmas Spirit and the whole Santa Claus thing. Each Christmas Eve, we would hang our stockings over the fireplace and place a small glass of milk and a plate of cookies on the mantelpiece for the fat man. We would then go to bed and listen for the sound of hooves on the roof and the jingle of bells. No kidding, we really did. We would stay awake in bed as long as we could but of course, exhaustion eventually won out and we would drift off to sleep.

However, at the crack of Dawn, and in Vermont in December, the crack of dawn came before the sun was up, especially on December 25th. In any case, we would get out of bed and go to our parent's room to see if they were awake. Nope, still asleep. Back to bed for what seemed to be an eternity but what in reality was probably only five minutes.

After a couple of these ups-and-downs, we made enough noise so that my parents got the message and got up. Mother would come into our rooms to make sure we stayed there and put on our bathrobes while my dad, brave soul that he was, quietly went downstairs to make sure that Santa had vacated the premises. My sister and I would sit at the top of the stairs waiting for my dad to give the all clear. There were some years when it seemed like he was down there forever, I mean, jeez, Santa is either there or gone. Finally, dad would call up, "Ok, you can come down now." Pounding down the stairs we went over to the piles of Santa's presents under our fireplace stockings.

One Christmas I will never forget, however, was the one where Santa really messed up. My sister and I were tearing through our Santa Claus goodies when I looked up and noticed the glass of milk and the small plate of cookies had not been touched. I turned around and said to my dad, "Hey, Santa did not drink his milk or eat his cookies." Dad quickly explained that Santa was probably too full of milk and cookies from his previous stops in the neighborhood. That satisfied me and I went back to going through my loot. However, I distinctly remember my mother giving my father what to me then was a funny look.Now, having been a parent myself and married for some forty-three years, I recall my mother's look and can easily translate it into, "Nice going, dummy". Good save on dad's part as both my sister and I bought it.

118

RECIPES

ere I add recipes for the day: both traditional and from a different country/culture. I hope that you will try a few of these recipes and perhaps incorporate them into your family traditions.

Monte Cristo Casserole

My almost-mother-in-law (unfortunately, I have a lot of those—Hi Evie!!) gave me this wonderful make-the-night-before breakfast casserole. It really does make the most awesome dish, and it is so easy to make.

Ingredients

- 1 cup skim milk

- 6 eggs

- 2 packs of Frozen French toast slices

- 8 oz. deli ham, diced into chunks

- 3 oz. deli turkey, diced into chunks

- 4 oz. Swiss cheese, grated, 1 cup

- ¼ cup fresh parsley, snipped

- 1/4 cup powdered sugar

- 2 cups fresh strawberries, sliced

- ½ cup strawberry ice cream topping

Directions

Preheat the oven to 375°F. Heat milk on HIGH for 3 minutes or until HOT. Whisk eggs in a small bowl; add hot milk to eggs, whisking until well blended. Cut French Toast into cubes, place in a large bowl. Pour the egg mixture over French Toast cubes, toss gently, and set aside. Combine ham, turkey, cheese and snipped parsley in a bowl. Mix. Layer half the French Toast cube at the bottom of the pan. Top with half the meat and cheese mixture. Repeat. Bake 30–35 minutes or until set in the center. Place in a cooling rack and sprinkle with powdered sugar.

Slice strawberries. Mix with the strawberry topping and heat in the microwave for 30 seconds. Cut the casserole into squares; serve using a spatula. Top each serving with strawberry mixture. You can also do the same thing with blueberries and blackberries. It is heavenly!!!! (For those of you who are curious, I had five almost-mother-in-laws. They ask me to marry them, I say yes (or maybe) and they run like hell. Very depressing.)

Sour Cream Apple Pie

My Nana is my dad's mother. She passed away before Thanksgiving last year and she is greatly, greatly missed. One of her many legacies is a fabulous cookbook my little sister put together for her of all our families favorite recipes. It was a huge undertaking and something we all cherish to this day; we are forever calling up the cousins and verifying a recipe and the question we always ask is: "Do you have Nana's cookbook?" In any case, one of my most favorite recipes and my dad's ULTIMATE favorite is Sour Cream Apple Pie.

Ingredients

- 1 cup sour cream

- 9-inch baked pie shell

- 2 tbsp, flour

- ¼ cup sugar

- 2 eggs

- 4 medium apples, peeled and sliced thinly

- 2 tsp. butter or oleo

- ½ cup sugar

- 1 tbsp, flour (yup, two uses)

- ½ tsp, cinnamon

Directions

To prepare the filling, combine and beat together the sour cream, flour, eggs, 1/4 cup of sugar and vanilla. Pare and core the apples then slice thinly. Fold the apples into the sour cream mixture and turn into pie crust. To prepare the topping, mix the last four ingredients in a small bowl, until it forms a crumbly mixture. Sprinkle over the pie and bake in a 350 °F oven for one hour.

Mints

This is a really fun activity to do with your kids as it is a very tactile recipe. You will need to buy some rubber candy molds in various shapes from Michaels or a candy supply shop. I bought mine from a very nice lady in Virginia who has since retired. This is a great activity to do around the kitchen table on a cold and frosty day. You can use the butter in two ways. One, don't melt it, keep it soft and place in a gallon zip lock bag to mix ingredients. This way, the kids can knead the bag and roll it around to mix the ingredients. If it's all adults, use the melted butter as shown in the recipe.

Ingredients

- 1 box powdered sugar (1 pound bag)

- 14 drops oil flavoring

- ½ stick butter softened or melted

- food coloring as needed

- 2 tablespoons hot water

- 1 cup granulated sugar

Directions

Mix melted butter, water, oil, flavoring, and coloring together in a bowl or zip-lock bag, your choice. Mix or knead carefully until well mixed. Roll into small balls the size of a marble (there's that marble again!) Press the ball of candy into the mold and unmold at once into a paper towel. Lay candies on a cookie sheet covered in wax paper. When all candies are done, place granulated sugar in a ziplock bag and put candies in with the sugar. Shake gently to coat candies. Remove and place back onto the cookie sheet. Let it set overnight in a cool, dark place. Store in the refrigerator or freezer. Makes a great Hostess gift!!!!

124

PUZZLES

```
F E A S T O F F O O L S Z Y
A S L U K E W R E I A I U Y
M A R K D T F E U I I A E I
A T D S L E P S O G R U O F
T U S D R I B Y L L O C J F
T R L A S R E V E R E L O R
H N D D Y A A N N L C U H N
E A O D I E V E B I P Y N N
W L V R D A U E A O Y R X N
I I D S E W J C A N E O Z F
E A B L A C K B I R D P I E
```

Blackbird Pie	John	Matthew
Colly Birds	Luke	Role Reversal
Feast of Fools	Mark	Saturnalia
Four Gospels		

CROSS STITCH DESIGN - SATURNALIA

 hese are designs for cross stitch patterns that you can use for ornaments, throws or dishcloths. They are a work in progress, so if you can improve upon the design, go for it!!! The patterns might not all be up by Christmas Time, so if the pattern isn't up this week, check back again.

128

COLORING PAGES/RED WORK DESIGN - AMERICAN SANTA

 hese are designs that can be used either for coloring pages for children or copied and transferred to cloth for Redwork for quilts. I kept the lines simple for both those reasons. Many of the designs have dots on them to show where to sew miniature bells or gold beads on them to represent jingle bells.

12 - United States - Santa Claus

From Shaman of the Winter Solstice to Saint Nicholas to (Saint Nick-Saint CLAUS) to Sinter Klaas to Sankte Klaus to the Final appellation thus far, the infamous Santa Claus. Ah, but it doesn't end there. He was also known in Germany as Pels Nickel or "Nicholas in Fur". That phrase came to America with the Germans in Dutch Pennsylvania and morphed into the name Belsnickle. This form of Santa was the precursor to the current jolly old elf… and was compared to the name Christkindle (bastardization of the name Krist Kind or Christ Child in German) so it went from Belsnickles to Christkindle to Kriskinckles to Kris Kringle. Ta Dah!!

Santa Claus underwent a huge transformation in a relatively short time period from scary shamanistic elf who wore old world robes and kept a sharp eye out for misbehaving children to the red clothed jolly ol' Saint Nick who kept track of children's deeds and rewarded them. This speedy transition was mainly due to the publication of "A Visit from St. Nicholas" by Clement Clarke Moore in 1823. Moore's poem took a figure that had survived thousands of years as a cult/shamanistic/religious figure and in almost one fell swoop, gave him over completely to the children. Santa Claus was theirs and theirs alone. HE existed solely because of and for them.

Thomas Nast gave a face to this character with his illustrations of Santa as a little, wizened, somewhat scary elf smoking a short pipe, symbol of the common man. (long stemmed pipes meant you were rich) This transformation became complete in 1930 when Fred Mizen painted the first Department Store Santa drinking a Coca-Cola. It appeared in the Saturday Evening Post in December 1930. It was an instant success, and in 1931 Coca-Cola hired Haddon Sundblom to paint Santa Claus with Coca-Cola products. For the next thirty-three years, Haddon Sundblom gave us the image of Santa we all know and love today, the snow white beard, the round, red cheeks, the red suit and black boots, the big belly and the knowing smile and the twinkle in his eye.

Note: Rudolph didn't come on the scene until 1939, when Robert L. May wrote the poem in the same meter as "Twas the Night Before Christmas". Years later, May's brother-in-law wrote the music for the song. It was sung first in 1948 by crooner Harry Brannon, and then later formally recorded by the singing cowboy himself, Gene Autry, 1949.

Santa Claus

Mele Kalikimaka

Hawaii

FIVE GOLDEN RINGS

> Five gold rings refer to ring-necked pheasants, not jewelry. The Romans inherited the pheasant from the Greeks and then brought it to England when they came a-conquering 2000 years ago.

The Five Gold Rings DO NOT refer to jewelry. They instead refer to ring-necked pheasants. The Romans inherited the pheasants from the Greeks and then brought it to England when they came a-conquering around 2000 years ago.

Also known as Boar's Head Day

The boar was sacred to the Celts and was associated with Gods and Mysteries in many parts of Northern Europe. Parading a boar's head around in procession was part and parcel of many medieval celebrations. Pigs were also a very important part of Medieval life, a mainstay in their diet. Pigs were often valued as much if not more than children, sharing the crowded and tiny huts in which they lived, both for protection from the elements and the predators.

BIBLICAL INTERPRETATION

The Five Gold Rings symbolize the first five testaments of the bible; telling of mans fall from grace.

he Five Gold Rings symbolize the first five Testaments of the Bible: The telling of man's fall from grace.

136

ANOTHER CULTURE'S WINTER CELEBRATION

Diwali
Oct-Nov Hindu

Diwali

The name "Diwali" is a contraction of Deepavali which translates into "row of lamps." Which is appropriate as it is a five-day Festival of Lights usually held between Mid-October and Mid-November. Diwali is popularly known as the "festival of lights," the most significant spiritual meaning is "the awareness of the inner light." Like the Muslim holiday of Ramadan, it is a focus on the "Spiritual Light Within." Central to Hindu philosophy is the belief that there is something beyond the physical body and mind which is pure, infinite, and eternal, called the Atman. The festival signifies the renewal of life; people wear new clothes on the day of the festival; it is a day of presents, sweets, dancing, families and good food. Fireworks are common after nightfall. Similarly, it heralds the approach of winter and the beginning of the sowing season.

In my hometown in North Carolina, a Diwali Festival was held on October 16th at a local amphitheater. Thousands turned out for the tenth Annual Festival of Lights. It was a beautiful fall day, and the colors of the trees were put to shame by the beautiful clothes the numerous dancers wore onstage. The food smells filling the air made your stomach growl nonstop and everywhere, children were running and laughing. I never knew how much I enjoyed curry and chickpeas until then. The dance programmes were amazing, and the afternoon was spent on a long sunny slope, eating curried chicken and chickpeas while watching some amazing performers.

Word Knerd

Is it all a numbers game? Almost every civilization has placed extreme importance on a certain number and how it figures into their daily lives. For example, there is this event called the Wild Hunt. In Norse/Germanic myths the leader of the Hunt is Odin/Wodan (See Wednesday). Wodan rides an eight-legged horse named Sleipnir. His companions were the Valkyries, and the honored dead who lived in Valhalla, the Great Hall of the Dead. The Hunt began on Winter's Night, (Halloween-October 31st) and went on until May's Eve (the day before May Day, April 30th). These two nights were known as nights where the spirits were free to roam the earth at will and do mischief as they wanted.

However, the height of the Hunt was, of course, Winter Solstice, December 21st, the Yule. Odin/Wodan is dressed as an old man with one eye, in blue robes, a long white beard, carrying a wooden staff and wearing a wide brimmed hat.

Seeing the Wild Hunt in the sky, a vision of ghostly horses and huntsmen, surrounded by baying dogs, careening about in the sky was supposed to be akin to the seeing of the Banshee of Ireland/Scotland. Seeing the Hunt or the Banshee was to know that Death itself was coming, war or impending catastrophe.

Numbers played (still do) an important part in Mythology. There are **twelve months** in the calendar year, agriculturally speaking, and most Yule Festivals, no matter what Culture, last about **twelve days,** beginning with the **Twelve-Day** Festival of Horus in Egypt on through the **twelve Days** of Christmas in Europe. Odin/Wodan rode a horse with eight legs (pretty fearsome looking) and Julnisse (Scandinavian Santa) rode a cart pulled by eight goats. **Reindeers** are a symbol of the Pagan god Herne, also a leader of a Wild Hunt. Santa's sleigh is pulled by **eight reindeer** (Rudolph, lucky number nine, came much later in the 1940s). **Eight** is a lucky number in China; it is the number of new beginnings and when laid on its side, eight is the symbol for Infinity.

TADA!!!!!!!

Books

Twinkling Lights, Diwali Nights
by Rupi K. Sandhu
ISBN-97815251833332

Lights for Gita by Rachna
Gilmore
ISBN-978-0-88448-151-5

140

REMEMBRANCES

hese are the stories I collected from my friends, family and people I met while traveling overseas, most notably from the Coalition Forces in Camp Bucca, Iraq. These stories are their most favorite memories of their Winter Celebrations and Traditions.

Eid - al - Adha

"Larry" Interpreter, Compound 16
Camp Bucca, Iraq

It is the most famous celebration day in Iraq and other Arabic countries. *Al Hajaj*, who they are going to visit *At-kahbah*, they go to Arafat Mountain. At this time, this is Al-Eid. It comes two months after Ramadan. There are four days in Eid. The families in Iraq prepare for this celebration. They clean their houses and put some flowers, like roses, and beautiful pictures on the walls inside the rooms.

Every year, my mother, sisters, even me, my father, and my brothers, help them to do jobs like clean furniture, TV, and make the place presentable. My mom and my sisters were always too busy to make sweet cake, candy, and clean the floor. We were still at work at three or four in the morning. Sometimes, we never slept.

So, at eight or nine o'clock, the people in my village come to celebrate at my home. They greet my father, my grandfather, my brothers, and me one by one by shaking their hands and kissing them. At this moment, my mom greets them and starts to give visitors sweet cake and candy. The famous phrase they greet us with is "Eidak Mobarek", and we answer with, "Ayamkom Saedah," and then the visitors enter inside the big hall. We have a very big hall in my home. All the people come to this hall to have coffee every day, because my grandfather is the Big Head of our tribe. My grandfather was always inside the Hall. They drink coffee and then eat "Bahatah," a popular Iraqi dish made of rice, milk, and sugar.

It is a very nice meal. In Iraq, it is customary for people to gather until noon, after which they typically return home or attend a banquet. This tradition stems from the practice of sacrificing a lamb during Eid al-Adha in honor of a deceased individual. In this custom, the bereaved family invites others to join them in this communal feast. Each deceased person is commemorated with seven sacrifices.

Every evening, our family comes to see us, bringing us delectable cakes, oranges, and apples as gifts. They stay for dinner, forming friendly groupings. The next day, as is customary, fellow villagers gather in our communal hall, where coffee is provided and new guests are welcomed, just like tribal chiefs do. The third day is dedicated to socializing with friends through games, puzzles, and riddles. My family and I spend Eid outside of town, visiting locations like the zoo or a park, before returning home at night. As the fourth day approaches, we begin cleaning up our home, bringing our holiday celebrations to a close.

RECIPES

ere I add recipes for the day: both traditional and from a different country/culture. I hope that you will try a few of these recipes and perhaps incorporate them into your family traditions.

Homemade Macaroni and Cheese with Ham

This whole season is about comfort food, and dinner isn't complete without macaroni and cheese! This is a simple, simple recipe and you can jazz it up with chunks of ham or bits of broccoli.

Ingredients

- 1 cup milk

- 1 ice cube of water/flour thickener

- 1 cup fresh shredded parmesan

- 1 cup each of shredded Cabot Vermont Cheddar, White American and your choice of flavored cheese. Or just three cups of shredded cheddar.

- 2 cups of your choice pasta

Directions

First, It's always a good idea to have a thickener on hand. I usually mix twelve tablespoons of water with twelve tablespoons of flour (cold water and add the flour to the water, not the other way around). Make sure it's mixed very well with no lumps. (Hey, looky!! Making glue again!)

Pour mixture into an ice cube tray and freeze. This way, if you ever need to thicken gravy or make a roux or white sauce, you can just throw in one of the cubes. It melts uniformly and is a quick fix. You can also freeze leftover wine the same way. Place ice cubes in a labeled paper brown bag in the freezer and they will never stick together. Another Nana trick.

Place one cup of milk in a small sauce pan. Heat gently; when bubbles start forming, start adding the cheeses GRADUALLY. Do not dump all the cheese in at one time. Stir constantly until well blend-

ed. Here, you can add broccoli bits or chunks of ham. Remove from heat and set aside. Boil up some water and throw in two cups of the pasta of your choice. When tender, drain, and fold gently into the cheese mixture. Sprinkle with fresh parmesan. Enjoy!

Chicken Curry Stew

Not a fan of curry. Never have been. Until my parents next door neighbors, also British, gave her a recipe for chicken salad. This recipe has peanut butter AND curry in it. So I tried it and it was great!! So I asked Claire, (next door neighbor) for the name of the curry and it was Schwartz' Mild Curry powder, another item you buy off of www.buybritish.net/store. There is another brand Waitrose Cooks Ingredients, C Brand, that is also nice and mild. I haven't found any American brands that are as smooth as mild as these.

In any case, there was a yummy recipe for curried chicken on the label of the Schwartz' brand and I used it to create a Chicken Curry Stew. Very good over rice or by itself.

Ingredients

- 3 Tbsp, oil

- 1 lb. chicken breasts, cubed

- 4 cups chicken broth

- 1 onion, finely chopped

- 2 Tbsp, curry powder

- 1 can diced tomatoes, 400 grams/14.5 oz

- 6 potatoes, peeled and cubed

- 3 carrots peeled and chopped

Directions

In a deep skillet, saute onions with olive oil, gradually add the two tablespoons curry powder. When well mixed, add the chicken and cook for around 5 minutes. Remove from heat. Put chicken broth into the slow cooker, add the vegetables and the chicken and onions mix. Put on low heat for around 7-8 hours. You can add more vegetables or take some out, it's your choice.

Enjoy!

Carrot Cake

I am not a cake person at all. Growing up I would always have Birthday Pie, not cake. But my little sister has a recipe that is to die for and I recommend it for anyone!

Kate's Carrot Cake - Not for the faint hearted or anyone watching their cholesterol!!!! ☺

Ingredients

- 2¼ cups flour

- 2 cups sugar

- 2 tsp. cinnamon

- 1 tsp. salt

- 2 tsp. baking soda

- 4 eggs

- 1 1/3 cups vegetable oil

- 3 cups grated carrots

- 1 cup chopped walnuts

- 1 cup (drained) crushed pineapple

- 1 cup shredded coconut

Cream cheese frosting

- 3 cups powdered sugar

- ¼ cup margarine

- ½ tsp. vanilla extra

- 8 oz. softened cream cheese

Directions

Stir together the dry ingredients in a large bowl. In another large bowl, mix together the eggs, oil, carrots, nuts, pineapple, and coconut. Add the wet mixture to the dry ingredients and mix well. Pour into a greased and floured 9x13 inch pan and bake for 45–50 minutes. Check doneness with a toothpick inserted in the center of the cake.

Allow to cool fully! This cake is very dense and takes a while to cool. Mix the frosting ingredients together in a deep bowl with an electric mixer. Frost cake and sprinkle with additional chopped walnuts if desired. Store cake in the refrigerator.

148

Day 5

PUZZLES

```
P W Z M E H R O C P Y E G O G G P U
E I U O I K O U H M D K E E U Q A G
U M A N S F A L L F R O M G R A C E
M W D I E S M E O Y A D E M I B A F
Y U F I V E G O L D E N R I N G S R
R I N G N E C K E D P H E A S A N T
M R D F I V E T E S T A M E N T S M
R K O A W S F D P M R R O M M N Y O
T Y G I E A A O Q G A E C R A Z F F
E V R L I H U C F A V U R L M A T E
R F E A L A S R F U Z Q Y M C J S I
E U E W A T T R E L I N Q D E N N O
F Q K I Z F E S A A O O U Q A P A U
Z D S D B D S E C O G C W K T I M O
X O L E I B E M U R B S A U B H O D
W D O E V R D N I P C O Z O D S R N
```

Boar's Head	Five Testaments	Man's Fall from Grace
Conquer	Greeks	Ring-Necked Pheasant
Diwali	Hindu	Romans
Five Golden Rings		

CROSS STITCH DESIGN - STOCKING

These are designs for cross-stitch patterns that you can use for ornaments, throws or dishcloths. They are a work in progress, so if you can improve upon the design, go for it!!! The patterns might not all be up by Christmas Time, so if the pattern isn't up this week, check back again.

COLORING PAGES/RED WORK DESIGN - SAINT NICHOLAS / BISHOP OF MYRA

 hese are designs that can be used either for coloring pages for children or copied and transferred to cloth for Red work for quilts. I kept the lines simple for both those reasons. Many of the designs have dots on them to show where to sew miniature bells or gold beads on them to represent jingle bells.

Saint Nicholas

Bishop
of Myra
270-343

11 – Europe – Saint Nicholas

Did you know Saint Nicholas became the Bishop of Myra simply because he was in the right place at the right time? Nicholas was born in 280 in Patara, Lycinia (Lycia) to Nonna and Epiphanius. Nicholas was very close to his Uncle Nicholas, a priest in Xanthos, and spent a lot of time with him. After his parents died, he went to live with his uncle in the Monastery. When he took his vows to become a monk, he was told he must dispose of his parent's wealth.

Here is where the legend of Santa begins:

A neighboring man had three daughters; however, he was very poor and unable to provide a proper dowry for them, thus condemning them to a life of spinsterhood, slavery or worse. Nicholas heard of this situation and sought to ease two burdens at once. He went to the man's house under the cover of night and when the house was asleep, reached in the window and tossed gold pieces into three stockings hanging by the fire to dry. He went away as silently as he had come, the daughters were saved and Nicholas was able to enter the Order. This was how the tradition of hanging stockings to be filled with presents began. (Patron Saint of Pawnbrokers, their symbol is three Golden Balls representing the three sisters' dowries)

The Bishops of Lycia gathered one year in Myra to choose a successor for Nicholas' uncle, as he was old and infirm. They couldn't agree on a man and finally decided in desperation to elect the next man who walked through the doors of the Church. Nicholas had an affinity for the sea and "for those who go down to the sea in ships," and it was while returning from one of his many voyages that he went to the Church to give thanks for a safe return. He walked through the doors and they clapped the Mitre hat on him and he became Bishop of Myra (Patron saint of Sailors).

In 325, Nicholas traveled with other Bishops to the Council of Nicaea where Constantine made the decree that Christs' Birthday would be celebrated on December 25th. Bishop Nicholas was made so angry at the words of Arius, a priest from Alexandria, that he slapped him in the face and was arrested and thrown in jail (Patron Saint of Thieves).

The custom of setting out shoes to be filled with candy and treats on the Eve of St. Nicholas Day (December 5th) started in the Netherlands. Holland was subject to Spain then, so Saint Nicholas was a Spanish Bishop. He is often depicted with a black servant, called Black Peter, as a representation of the Moorish slaves of the Spanish Dominion. This is where the legend of Santa's Helpers or "elves" began. Saint Nicholas, Bishop of Myra, died in 344.

156

SIX GEESE A-LAYING

The goose is the symbol of the solar year and the solstice as it disappears in the fall and returns in the spring. It is also the symbol of fertility and rebirth

 he goose is the symbol of the solar year and the Winter Solstice as the sun disappears in the Fall and returns full strength in the Spring. It is also the symbol of fertility and rebirth.

Also known as New Year's Eve or Hogmanay.

157

158

Day 6

BIBLICAL INTERPRETATION

The Six Geese
A-Laying
symbolize the
six days of
creation.

 he Six Geese A-Laying symbolize the six days of Creation.

160

ANOTHER CULTURE'S WINTER CELEBRATION

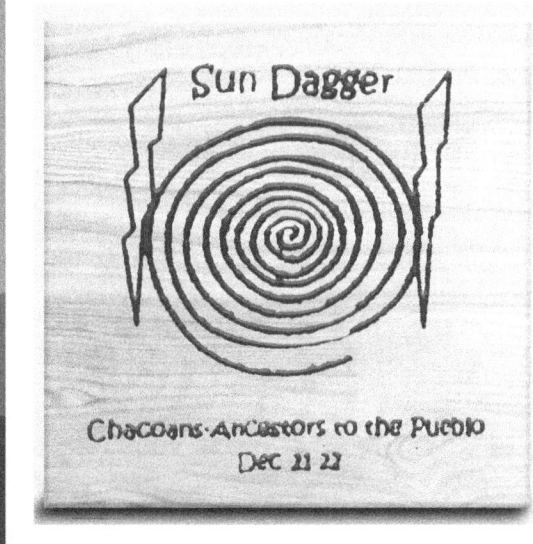

Native Americans have winter solstice rites. There are the Chumash, who occupied coastal California for thousands of years before the Europeans arrived. Solstices were tremendously important to them, and the winter solstice celebration lasted several days. The Chacoans, ancestors to the Pueblo Indians of the Southwest, created awesome calendars to mark the moments of both Winter and Summer Solstice. Their Winter Solstice Festivals were filled with bonfires, dances, traditional foods and gift giving.

In 1977, an artist named Anna Sofaer was exploring some rock art in the Southwest, and she came upon a light pattern playing upon the walls of Fajada Butte around four hundred feet above the canyon floor. Carved into the wall beneath three slabs of sandstone leaning against the walls are two spirals, one large and one small. At certain times of the year, the sun pours through the slabs to create patterns on the spirals that resemble daggers. For the Winter Solstice, two daggers bookend the larger spiral, which had nine lines. For the Summer Solstice, a single dagger pierces the center. For the Equinoxes, the Vernal and the Autumnal, a dagger pierces between the 4th and 5th ring on the larger spiral and directly through the heart of the smaller spiral. Unfortunately, in the 1980s, natural occurrences shifted the stones and the calendar no longer functions. But, what an amazing timepiece! Something hundreds upon hundreds of years old, carved to mark the most important days of the year, so that important spiritual matters could be attended to properly.

Winter Solstice

Many Native Americans hold to the Old Ways, yet many others have converted to Christianity, and as is the way of different cultures existing close to one another, traditions blend and grow. Some adhere to the traditional Santa figures and stories. Others have come up with their own and he is known as "Old Red Shirt". He is a Native American Shaman figure, Santa-like in that he travels around to all the good little boys and girls in a sled pulled by eight white buffalo. The focus of this Santa is not only that boys and girls have been good but also if they have been good to others. Read "Native American Night Before Christmas" by Gary Robinson for a complete retelling; the illustrations by Jesse Hummingbirds are so colorful and gorgeous!!!!

Word Knerd

Latin	Germanic/Norse Gods	Spanish	English
Dies Mercuri	Woden/Odin or Woden's Day	Miercoles	Wednesday

Books

Thirteen Moons on Turtle's Back: A Native American Year of Moons by Joseph Bruchac & Jonathan London and illustrated by Thomas Locker
ISBN-9780698115842

Native American Night Before Christmas by Gary Robinson and illustrated by Jesse Hummingbird
ISBN-9781574160932

164

 Day 6

REMEMBRANCES

hese are the stories I collected from my friends, family and people I met while traveling overseas, most notably from the Coalition Forces in Camp Bucca, Iraq. These stories are their most favorite memories of their Winter Celebrations and Traditions.

A Yuletide Happening

Carleen R.
Saraland, AL

Hello, I thought I would send you this Yuletide Happening. My people are Celtic and Northern European and American Indian. They settled in Northwest Alabama. They saw hardship, famine and the Trail of Tears. They went through both the Colonial and Civil Wars, as well as WW1 and WW2. From early on, I knew about gifts and strange happenings. I knew I was not a Christian. But there were no others, at least none that would share with me. I was in Northwest Alabama and there this one thing happened to cement my Pagan-ness.

This happened to my Papow Burton. He was born in 1901. He had seen Halley's Comet twice in his lifetime. He had only a second grade education as he was a simple sharecropper farmer. He didn't go to church much but he was much loved.

Well, when my father retired from the Army in 1976, we moved back to Cullman, Alabama. We, my brother and I, got to spend more time with our grandparents. So we were all gathered at Mammow's and Papow's house. A tradition was to give Papow a small bottle of liquor, Jack Daniels or Wild Turkey. Well, Mammow had made Papow stop brewing moonshine and beer and wine. He was always in pain. His spine and ribs were a solid mass caused by age and rheumatism. So, as usual, he drank his little bottle up then went out to take a walk with his dogs. Papow always reminded me of the master of the Hounds. That was one of his gifts, dogs loved him. He had at that time twenty-one dogs of different sizes and shapes. He had made it to the woodshed when he looked up to see an Angel. He said it told him that he was blessed with a long life, that he has things yet to do. Well, when he told everyone, they all laughed and said he had drunk too much.

But later, someone else told him that they had seen the same thing. That someone was me. I was in the backroom when I happened to look outside through a window. I thought it was strange, every dog was sitting around Papow looking up. All twenty-one of them. Papow was looking up too. The figure had fair hair and was shone in a light. Papow said he was an Angel. I told him he was one of the fair Folk!! The Sidhe. But in later years, it only confirmed these thoughts with other happenings. I am still a Pagan, an Asatru A'r with strong Celtic ties.

These may not be fourth grade tales, but I wanted my Papow to be remembered, him and his dogs and his Angel, in these changing times.

A Wiccan Yule Memory

Blessed Be and Blessings on your wonderful project.
- Morgan

Hello!

I happened to read your ad in Sage Woman and couldn't help but drop you a line. I was raised as an Orthodox Jew until age thirteen when I found my first "teacher" and began my walk on the Pagan path, much to my mother's horror. But even though we were painfully poor (she never counted on being a single parent in the sixties), I remember Yule holidays when she gave up coffee and cigarettes so I could have a few presents under the "Hanukkah Bush," even though that was her main sustenance at the time. But the one thing we always managed to do, no matter how broke she was, was to take whatever form of cookies she was trying that year to the local ER, cop shop, and fire department. It was sort of her Kharmic way of stacking up good will in hopes of not needing their services in the upcoming year.

She died when I was sixteen, the same year I graduated from High school. Since I only had enough scholarship money and time to pull off a two year degree to be able to support myself at age eighteen, I first became a nurse and then I ended up working ALL the holidays so those with kids could be at home with them. Not once during all those long night shifts did anyone ever bring us goodies; after all—we were being paid to do our jobs, why should we expect more? I actually had a patient's wife say that to me mere moments after I saved her husband's life. I swore to myself I would change that lack of human comfort. When my own children were born, I restarted the tradition. As my family grew, so did the number of places we stopped.

Every Christmas/Solstice Eve, instead of fighting to get them into bed, I would bundle all of them up (there ended up being six of them), and out we'd go. Even when I chose to become a single Mom, the tradition continued no matter how broke I was. Even if it was only "slice & bake" decorated cookies, out we went into the night to all the places most people never think about during those lonely holiday hours.

The emergency room, the fire department, the local police station, and if I was flush with cash for a change, the local nursing home, and the homeless shelter. It wasn't much. Some fudge, a few cookies, some applesauce raisin cake and a few candy canes, but the look in the eyes of the people we gave them to was worth its weight in gold, and I think it made my kids more appreciative of all those who may not have been able to be at home or may not have a home to go to. When I married my soulmate almost ten years ago, this was the one tradition that amazed him the most. He had never had a "real" holiday like ours before. If my life as a child was bleak, his was dissolute. The fact that our first real holiday together was in a tiny trailer in a dust bowl town in New Mexico, and we were too broke to pay attention, he was amazed that my kids still wanted to do something nice for other people even though they knew it would mean fewer gifts for them under the Solstice tree—it was okay.

I really think that first Holiday was what melted the heart of this wonderful man who swore he hated kids, marriage, and most especially HOLIDAYS. When they were little, the trip always ended with someone spotting a blinking red light in the sky (some stray radio tower) and declaring that we had to go home RIGHT NOW because the Big Guy in the red suit was flying overhead. Never had a fight to get them to bed after that! ☺ Two of my four daughters are married now, one working, one becoming a paramedic, and I know that even though they are all out on their own now, they still hold that tradition dear. They may only offer to work someone else's shift so they can be home to tuck a little one in bed, but they all still pass out goodies to the locals who keep us safe through the year, even if they happen to be co-workers.

My husband and I make the rounds even though it's just us now, and it's still his favorite part of the season. We drag along whatever friends are around and we know we've spread the habit to more than a few of them. After all, isn't that what this time of year is all about? Bringing a little light into the darkness to those who need it the most?

Day 6

RECIPES

 ere I add recipes for the day: both traditional and from a different country/culture. I hope that you will try a few of these recipes and perhaps incorporate them into your family traditions.

Coca-Cola Stew

Now, this is a recipe I got from eavesdropping. I was on the treadmill at the gym, in the eternal quest for my waist, when I overheard my sweaty neighbor chatting to HER sweaty neighbor about this awesome recipe she just tried. I listened closely, and it seemed pretty darn easy and pretty good. I like easy. So, here you go:

Ingredients

- 2 lbs. beef tips/stew meat

- 1 16 oz. bottle Coca-Cola

- 1 packet onion soup mix

- 4 carrots, peeled and chopped

- 1 large onion, diced

- several stalks of celery, chopped

- 6 potatoes, peeled and chopped

- 2 thickener cubes

- 1 can diced tomatoes (400 grams/14.5 oz)

- ½ small head cabbage, shredded

Directions

Place shredded cabbage or meat into the crock pot. Mix together onion soup mix and Coca-Cola, and pour over meat and cabbage. Mix well, cover and let sit overnight in the fridge. The Coca-Cola breaks down any tough fibers in the meat and totally tenderizes the cabbage too.

Peel and chop vegetables the night before.

The next morning, add your vegetables to the crock pot, pour in the can of diced tomatoes and the chicken broth and mix well. Cover and set on LO for eight hours.

Bread Pudding

This is another Nana favorite. You can make it the night before and pop it in the oven in the morning. Hot bread pudding with maple syrup is a great way to start the day!!! I call this my 1-2-3-4 recipe.

Ingredients

- 1 teaspoon vanilla

- 2 cups milk

- 3 eggs

- 4 cups cubed bread

- Raisins to taste

Directions

Mix the eggs with milk and beat well. Mix in the vanilla. Add some raisins if you like, at this point. Pour over the bread cubes and mix well. Pour into a loaf pan and shape. Let it sit in the refrigerator overnight or bake immediately. Preheat the oven to 350°F and bake for 30 minutes until golden brown. Take out and set on the stove to cool. Slice and serve.

There is a nice alternative called Puerto Rican Bread Pudding. Substitute the regular bread with a loaf of cornbread and use half a cup of coconut milk with a splash of rum in addition to the one cup regular milk. Add some more bread cubes if need be.

Baked Pineapple

This is a family staple at every Holiday table. Before you go "Ew!!!! Cheese and pineapple?!?! Think about a Hawaiian pizza. 'Nuff said.

Ingredients

- 1½ cups sugar

- 6 Tbsp flour

- 6 Tbsp pineapple juice

- 2 20-oz cans of pineapple chunks, drained except for 6 tbsp.

- 2 cups Shredded Cheese

- 2 cups Ritz crackers (crushed)

- 1 stick butter (1/2 cup) melted

Directions

Combine sugar, flour and pineapple juice in a small pan. Heat on LO until the sugar melts. Stir in pineapple and cheese. Pour into a baking dish, top with Ritz crackers, and drizzle with melted butter. Preheat the oven to 350°F and bake for 25–30 minutes. You will be asked to make this again and again!

174

Day 6

PUZZLES

```
D Q T X A S O L A R Y E A R K U W
Y V E I G G S O T N K L Y D P N Q
J C Z H T R I B E R Y M T X E S R
B A O I N H E R E D M G C B H E A
N E W Y E A R S E V E P V Y G O Z
E T O P F E R T I L I T Y G U P A
I E E D E H J C E M R I A A I Y I
H V D T H A F M W Q E D C O M X V
C H A C O C A N Y O N O F D R G V
C V S A F S O P O U U H Y A N Q C
D I E R I G E E S E A L A Y I N G
S I X D A Y S O F C R E A T I O N
U X A I E M Y O V N W E S O O G D
R C C R J I S P U E B L O C O I C
U O M A A U S M N P F I G N O P P
```

Chaco Canyon	New Year's Eve	Six Days of Creation
Fertility	Pueblo	Solar Year
Geese A Laying	Rebirth	Sun Dagger
Goose		

CROSS STITCH DESIGN - CHACO SOLSTICE CARVING

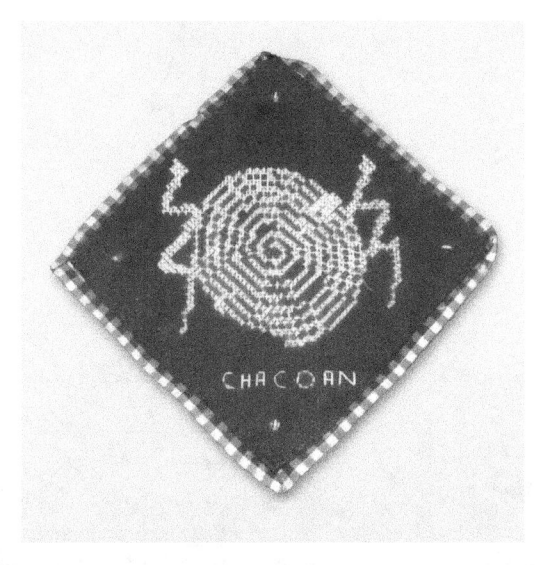

hese are designs for cross stitch patterns that you can use for ornaments, throws or dishcloths. They are a work in progress, so if you can improve upon the design, go for it!!! The patterns might not all be up by Christmas Time, so if the pattern isn't up this week, check back again.

178

COLORING PAGES/RED WORK DESIGN - OLD RED SHIRT / NATIVE AMERICAN SANTA

 hese are designs that can be used either for coloring pages for children or copied and transferred to cloth for Redwork for quilts. I kept the lines simple for both those reasons. Many of the designs have dots on them to show where to sew miniature bells or gold beads on them to represent jingle bells.

Old Red
Shirt

Native American

4 - Native America - Old Red Shirt

The Native American Santa Claus is known as "Old Red Shirt" as Native Americans do not have a word for Santa Claus, instead giving endearing names to people based on their appearance or their actions. As many cultures have throughout the world, Native Americans across the United States have adopted Santa Claus and made him their own.

In a book written by Gary Robinson and illustrated by Jesse Hummingbird, you can read a beautiful remake of The Night Before Christmas and look at gorgeous brightly colored illustrations of Old Red Shirt and his eight white buffalo. They are called, "Harjo, Red Bow, Chino, Kola, Tallchief, White Cloud, Sam and Yahola and he calls to them with a hearty Hoka-hey!!

Lakota warriors used to shout Hoka-hey to each other as they charged into battle; today Elders use it as a term of encouragement. As with many cultures who have adopted Santa Claus, the Native Americans' Old Red Shirt stresses the importance of giving rather than receiving and the importance of being with Family at this special time.

182

SEVEN SWANS A-SWIMMING

Ancient people were fascinated by waterfowl because they could swim, dive and fly. They associated flying with the spirit world. In ancient Egypt the swan is associated with immortality and in England it is a symbol of royalty.

ncient people were fascinated by waterfowl because they could swim, dive and fly. They associated flying with the spirit world. In Ancient Egypt the swan is associated with immortality and in England it is associated with Royalty.

Also known as First Footing Day and Wassailing Day

First Footing Day is mostly celebrated in Scotland but is observed in almost all of the UK. First Footing is New Year's Day, and the First Foot to cross over the threshold of any household on this day HAD to be a person with dark hair or the year would be unlucky. This goes back to Viking times in Britannia, when most visitors to the island were not welcome and were mostly of the invading sort. Big, blond, and generally unpleasant, they would rape, pillage and loot their larcenous little guts out. So the tradition grew to where blonds were NOT known as having more fun. At least not to the Scots. Yet another tradition for this day when you go visiting on New Year's Day, which is when families go and see one another, is to bring the following items:

- A wee dram of whiskey—so that the house would not know thirst the rest of the year.

- A lump of coal—so that the house would always have fuel and be warm and welcoming.

- A piece of shortbread—so that the house would never know hunger.

- A penny—So that the house would not know poverty.

These gifts, in various combinations, were brought as a measure of good will and wishes for the year to come.

Waes Hael in Old English means "be whole" or "be well". Wassail is a medieval drink made of mulled ale, curdled cream, roasted apples, eggs, cloves, ginger, nutmeg and sugar. The Wassail drink mixture was sometimes called 'Lamb's Wool', because the pulp of the roasted apples looked all frothy and a bit like lamb's wool!!!

One of the traditions was to go a-wassailing, meaning going around singing to your neighbors and begging for a bit of a drink and a treat. It was also meant to take a bowl of the wassail and go into the orchards. Bread soaked in apple cider would be thrown into the branches and wassail poured onto the tree's roots as a sort of sacrifice to the trees. I always thought that was a little creepy, myself, pouring bits of hot juice of an apple back onto and into the apple tree as an offering seemed a little cannibalistic. Weapons were fired into the air to scare off bad spirits and songs were sung to aid the trees in a bountiful spring and a good harvest in the year to come.

One of the most popular Wassailing Carols :

Here we come a-wassailing
Among the leaves so green,
Here we come a-wassailing,
So fair to be seen:

Love and joy come to you,
And to you your wassail too,
And God bless you and send you,
A happy New Year.

BIBLICAL INTERPRETATION

The Seven Swans A-Swimming symbolize the seven gifts of the Holy Spirit: wisdom, understanding, right judgement, courage, knowledge, and reverence and awe in his presence.

The Seven Swans a-Swimming symbolize the seven gifts of the Holy Spirit: Wisdom, Understanding, Right Judgement, Courage, Knowledge, and Reverence in His Presence.

186

ANOTHER CULTURE'S WINTER CELEBRATION

Kwanzaa

Kwanzaa was created by Ron Karenga back in the 1960s and is a week-long African-American festival primarily honoring African-American heritage. It is observed from December 26 to January 1 each year. The name Kwanzaa derives from the Swahili phrase *"matunda ya kwanza"* meaning "first fruits". The emphasis of this Holiday is family and community. One of the phrases used a lot is *"Habari Gani!"* meaning "What is the News?" or our current day translation "What's up?"

The following are the *"Nguzo Saba"* or the seven principles of community.

- *Umoja* (Unity): To strive for and maintain unity in the family, community, nation, and race.

- *Kujichagulia* (Self-Determination): To define ourselves, name ourselves, create for ourselves and speak for ourselves.

- *Ujima* (Collective Work and Responsibility): To build and maintain our community together and make our brothers' and sisters' problems our problems and to solve them together.

- *Ujamaa* (Cooperative Economics): To build and maintain our own stores, shops and other businesses, and to profit from them together.

- *Nia* (Purpose): To make our collective vocation the building and developing of our community in order to restore our people to their traditional greatness.

- *Kuumba* (Creativity): To always do as much as we can, in the way we can, in order to leave our community more beautiful and beneficial than we inherited it.

- *Imani* (Faith): To believe with all our heart in our people, our parents, our teachers, our leaders and the righteousness and victory of our struggle.

Word Knerd

The history of the word Thursday

Latin	Germanic/Norse Gods	Spanish	English
Dies Joves	Thor or Thor's Day	Jueves	Thursday
Day of Jupiter			

Books

'Twas the Night Before
Christmas
by Melodye Rosales and
Clement Moore
ISBN-9780590739443

The Night Before Christmas in
Africa by Jesse Foster, Hannah
Foster, and Carroll Foster
ISBN-9781589808515

K is for Kwanzaa: A Kwanzaa
Alphabet Book by Juwanda G. Ford
illustrated by Ken Wilson-Max
ISBN-9780613722261

190

REMEMBRANCES

wans-a-Swimming

These are the stories I collected from my friends, family and people I met while traveling overseas, most notably from the Coalition Forces in Camp Bucca, Iraq. These stories are their most favorite memories of their Winter Celebrations and Traditions.

Reminiscences of Hogmanay in Scotland in the Late Forties/Early Fifties

Cathy H. Fuquay
Varina, North Carolina

Christmas wasn't a big thing in Scotland in those days, although it has changed now. Children got a few presents but otherwise not much happened. The big day was Hogmanay, and all the family were involved in that.

As children we were put to bed early on New Year's Eve, and then we were woken up at about 11:30 in the evening to join the adults and the party, which could go on all night, until breakfast. New Year's Day was a public holiday so people didn't have to go to work.

Some people would be having a sort of 'open house' whilst others went round the neighborhood from party to party, and they were known as the 'first footers', although the first person through your door after midnight was the official first footer, and you wanted it to be a tall, dark haired man. He would carry a piece of coal 'to warm your fire for the rest of the year', and whisky. Everyone who was walking around from party to party would carry whisky to share, and all the parties would have a good supply of whisky too, and food to soak it all up. I'm not sure how people decided whether they would be giving a party or going round to others, but it seemed to be the people with younger children who would stay home and have open house, and older teenagers who would be walking the streets and knocking on doors—if you saw a light shining you could feel free to go in and party, as long as you had some whisky with you! Somehow it all worked out.

The food was just the normal buffet food, with lots of shortbread, as this was thought to be particularly good at soaking up the alcohol.

Everyone at the party was expected to 'do their turn,' that is sing a song, do a dance, recite a poem, tell a funny story or whatever. As my dad had been a singer with a dance band, he was always popular at parties. I attempted to sing too, but wasn't quite as successful! In fact none of us really lived up to his standards when it came to entertainment.

There would be lots of dancing and an accordion player usually turned up at your party which helped it go with a swing.

On New Year's day we children were expected to keep pretty quiet, as there were a lot of hangovers around, so the shortbread didn't work that well.

Three Christmas Trees

David H.
(My dad again, he LOVES Christmas!!!)
Windsor, Vermont

When I was a kid, I mean around the age of 7 to 14, I was really into Christmas. Not so much for decorations, or the pain of saving up money for buying gifts, trying to figure out what to buy for wrapping, etc. Nor did it have anything to do with the midnight Mass at the Church, Baby Church, or Joseph, Mary, the Magi, yadda, yadda, yadda. Nope, it was all about the presents I got. The loot, the goodies, the stuff under the tree marked, "To David" from "Who Cares."

One reads stories about kids who were born into a poor family who were lucky to get one present and that one present might have been a hand-me-down from an older sister or brother who had got the same gift the year before. I guess I was one lucky kid because I got to attend three Christmas Tree events.

On Christmas Eve, we would go over to my mother's parents' home in New Hampshire and open presents there. I always remember that Christmas Tree because they had those tree ornaments that had water in them which bubbled up when they warmed up. Christmas morning we had our own tree at our house in Windsor. Not only the tree, but that was where Santa came and he always left filled stockings hanging from the fireplace mantle plus presents underneath the stockings. After a late breakfast or an early lunch it was off to my dad's parents' home in downtown Windsor for another tree and more goodies for me.

Okay, so later in life, I gradually began to appreciate the wisdom of the saying, "Tis better to give than to receive" and take pleasure in watching someone open a gift that you purchased for them. But when I was a youngster, oh yeah, goodies for Dave! ☺

194

RECIPES

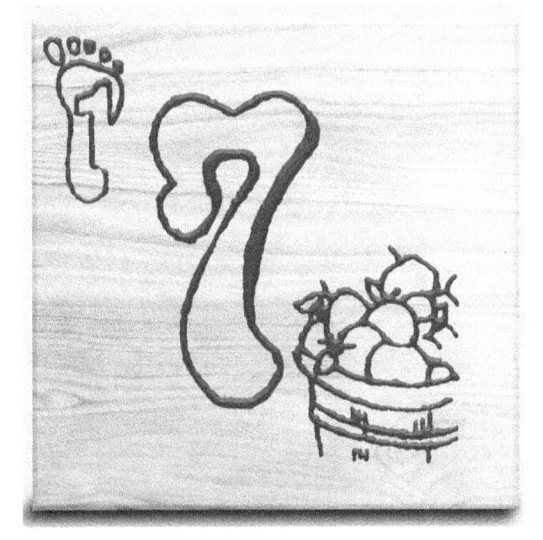

 ere I add recipes for the day: both traditional and from a different country/culture. I hope that you will try a few of these recipes and perhaps incorporate them into your family traditions.

Groundnut Stew

You will need around two cups of chopped peanuts. Soak half of them in hot pepper oil overnight. Leave the other half as garnish after the stew is done.

Ingredients

- 3 Tbsp. oil

- 1 lb. chicken breasts, cubed

- 4 cups chicken broth

- 1 onion, finely chopped

- 2 Tbsp, curry powder

- ½ cup crunchy peanut butter

- 1 can diced tomatoes (400 grams/14.5 oz)

- 6 potatoes, peeled and cubed

- 3 carrots peeled and chopped

Directions

In a deep skillet, sauté onions with olive oil, gradually add the two tablespoons of curry powder. When well mixed, add the chicken and cook for around 5 minutes. Remove from heat. Put chicken broth into the slow cooker, add the vegetables and the chicken and onions mix. Blend it with a half cup of peanut butter. Drain the peanuts from the hot pepper oil and add to the mix. Put on LO heat for around 7-8 hours. You can add more vegetables or take some out, it's your choice. Serve hot and garnish with the finely chopped peanuts. Enjoy!

Cream Puffs

Now, Martha Stewart (a moment of reverent silence, please) had this beautiful project in one of her magazines where she had cream puffs made in the shape of swans swimming in a pond of chocolate. Nice homage to the seven Swans, eh? Well, I can't do the swan shape here without running into copyright issues and stuff, but I do have a killer recipe from my mom for foolproof (shut up, Dad!) cream puffs. Mom puts both vanilla and chocolate cream inside and tops them with a chocolate ganache. Now, if YOU want to shape them like swans and pour Hershey' syrup on a saucer when serving them, that's totally on you.

Ingredients

- 1 cup water

- ½ cup butter or margarine

- ¼ tsp. salt

- 1 cup all sifted flour

- 4 large eggs

- vanilla/choc cream filling

Directions

Preheat the oven to 400°F.

In a saucepan, heat water, butter, and salt to a full roiling boil. Reduce the heat and quickly stir in the flour, stirring constantly. The mixture will form a ball and leave the sides of the pan. Remove from the heat and beat in the eggs one at a time. Using an electric mixer will ensure a smooth mix. Drop spoonfuls of the mixture onto a greased cookie sheet. Place cream puffs about three inches apart. You can make them any shape you want (You GO Martha Stewart fans!!!)

Bake for 10 minutes then lower the temperature to 350°F and continue baking for another 25 minutes. TURN OFF oven. Remove puffs from the oven and slit the sides of each puff and then put them back in the TURNED OFF oven for another 10 minutes. Cream puffs are done when they are firm to the touch, double in size and a golden brown.

Let cool. Slit the top and fill each cream puff with vanilla cream or chocolate cream. Drizzle with chocolate ganache. Makes about 12-16 cream puffs.

Chocolate Ganache

Ingredients

- 8 oz. bag of semi-sweet chocolate chips

- 1 cup heavy cream

Directions

Heat cream in a small saucepan; when in a hot simmer, gradually add chocolate chips. Stir until all melted. Let cool for 10 minutes before pouring over cream puffs.

Cream Filling

Ingredients

- 3 cups milk

- ¾ cup sugar

- 6 Tbsp. cornstarch

- ½ tsp. salt

- 3 eggs, beaten

- 1 Tbsp, butter

- 2 tsp. vanilla extract

Directions

Scald milk on the top part of a double boiler over boiling water. Mix sugar, cornstarch, and salt. Stir into the milk. Keep stirring until it thickens. Cover and cook for 10 minutes longer. Add a small amount of mixture to the eggs and stir vigorously. Keep adding more and more of the mixture to the eggs until they are all mixed together. Add butter and vanilla. Chill for 15 minutes before filling the cream puffs.

Chocolate Cream Filling:

For chocolate cream filling, melt three ounces of unsweetened chocolate in the milk and beat until smooth. Continue with the recipe as above.

Shortbread

This is one of the MUST HAVE gifts when you go visiting on First Footing Day. It is supposed to symbolize that the family receiving the gift will be blessed with plentiful food in the coming year.

Ingredients

- 1 cup butter, (unsalted, never cook with salted butter, it throws off the chemistry of the dish)

- ½ cup sugar

- 2 ½ cups all purpose flour

- ½ teaspoon vanilla (or not...your choice)

Directions

Mix all ingredients together, and the mixture should be crumbly. Press into a 9x12 baking pan. Use a fork to puncture the surface with dots all over the top of the shortbread. Preheat the oven to 325°F and bake for 30 minutes. Let cool and cut into shortbread fingers. To serve with style, melt some chocolate chips in the microwave and dip one end of each finger into the chocolate. Lay onto wax paper to cool.

202

PUZZLES

```
O Y I U A W A S S A I L U J A M A A A
S T E E I U A D L R O W T I R I P S L
T I M R O I M W D H S E F D U F Y Y I
F L U M I F I R S T F O O T I N G A K
I A S K S R J A P S M V S A I B E C E
G T I A Y U U R E V E R E N C E O A Z
N R P R P S W A N S A S W I M M I N G
E O C U R P Q L O E G A R U O C N C U
V M F Y Y U L K U J I C H A G U L I A
E M K N O W L E D G E U A I K M Y N S
S I E O U K C B S N M Z N U K N O N H
V F E A I I F Y E O N A U M O N B F Y
O Y T L A Y O R J A M M L H T A N I T
N R E G A B E A W I B J L R Y X W U Z
I W I S D O M K C A T N E M E G D U J
A U N D E R S T A N D I N G H O Y H O
```

Apples	Courage	Imani	Judgement
Kujichagulia	Kwanzaa	Reverence	Seven Gifts
Swans a Swimming	Ujima	Understanding	Wisdom
Awe	First Footing	Immortality	Knowledge
Kuumba	Nia	Royalty	Spirit World
Ujamaa	Umoja	Wassail	

CROSS STITCH DESIGN-THE KINARA

These are designs for cross stitch patterns that you can use for ornaments, throws or dishcloths. They are a work in progress, so if you can improve upon the design, go for it!!! The patterns might not all be up by Christmas Time, so if the pattern isn't up this week, check back again.

COLORING PAGES/RED WORK DESIGN -KENTE CLAUS AND RASTA SANTA / AFRICAN AMERICAN SANTA CLAUS

 hese are designs that can be used either for coloring pages for children or copied and transferred to cloth for Redwork for quilts. I kept the lines simple for both those reasons. Many of the designs have dots on them to show where to sew miniature bells or gold beads on them to represent jingle bells.

207

Kente
Claus
Afro-Am

Rasta Claus
Bahamas

209

7 - United States - Kente Claus

Kente Claus was created from the desire to allow children of all backgrounds to share in the wonderment of Santa Claus. He is depicted dressed in Kente cloth, the royal heritage cloth of Ghana in West Africa, and carries a stick made from the *Baobob* tree, representing strength and wisdom. He travels with a big black dog as a guardian, representing security. He has been shown in numerous modes of transportation, from a wagon being drawn by Okapis (a striped African animal related to the giraffe) to riding elephants, although no one illustrator has nailed down one image as of yet. As with many other Santas adapted into various cultures, Kente Claus stresses giving more than receiving and participating in supporting the community.

Kente Claus is part of a larger effort to provide children and adults with much-needed, positive African-American figures during the holidays.

EIGHT MAIDS A-MILKING

Refers to the many products of milk used in medieval times, mainly cheese which was a much valued food in winter. Asking a maid to go a-milking was the same as asking her to get married.

ight Maids A-Milking refers to the many products of milk used in Medieval Times, mainly cheese which was a much valued food in winter time. Asking a maid to go a-milking was somewhat licentious, actually one step further than the 50's version of parking, submarine races or today's "hooking up." It meant you were fooling around.

Also known as Snow Day

212

BIBLICAL INTERPRETATION

The Eight Maids A-Milking symbolize the eight beatitudes which mark the opening of the Sermon on the Mount.

he Eight Maids A-Milking symbolize the Eight Beatitudes which mark the opening of the Sermon on the Mount.

ANOTHER CULTURE'S WINTER CELEBRATION

St. Lucia Dec 13 Sweden

Saint Lucia Day - LuciaFest: The Festival of Lights

On Saint Lucia Day in Sweden, in households all over the country, the oldest daughter wakes up in the morning and puts on a white dress with a red sash. She puts a wreath on her head that holds five candles that symbolize the days growing longer with the growing light and then proceeds to serve her family coffee and saffron infused breakfast rolls called LusserKasse, little sweet rolls made yellow with saffron and shaped like a little cat with raisins for eyes. There are also pepparkakor or ginger snaps.

One of the oldest fables tells the beginnings of Lucia like this. The darkest day of the year, December 21st. symbolized the chance of starvation and death with its lack of food and the dark nights and brutal cold. There came a glow on the horizon of Lake Vaettern. Soon a longship appeared, with a blond maiden in a long flowing gown at the helm, and filled with food and supplies. The arrival of the ship staved off starvation for another year and the young girl came to symbolize the hope of light and growth for a new year.

Word Knerd

Latin	Germanic/Norse Gods	Spanish	English
Dies Venere	Frigga or Frigga's Day	Viernes	Friday
Day of venus			

Books

Lucia and the Light
by Phyllis root
ISBN-9780763622961

Lucia Saint of Light by
Katherine Bolger Hyde and
illustrations by Daria Fisher
ISBN-9780982277041

REMEMBRANCES

 hese are the stories I collected from my friends, family and people I met while traveling overseas, most notably from the Coalition Forces in Camp Bucca, Iraq. These stories are their most favorite memories of their Winter Celebrations and Traditions.

Story from an Almost Grinch

Vance "Quasimoto"
Minneapolis, Minnesota

How are you doing over there, kid? Are you having all the fun you can handle?

I have a few minutes at the moment and thought I'd donate a little to your Christmas book.

For as many years as I can remember, my family has done the exact same thing gastronomically on xmas eve. We do a steak fondue with various sides and lefse is always a staple. Amongst other nationalities we have a strong Norwegian background and that is where the lefse comes in. Frequently there will be herring as a precursor to the meal. I suppose one could call it an appetizer.

Anyway, we have our meal and then do the dishes afterwards. I'm usually one of the first ones done each year and will start the dishes after I've had a chance to relax and enjoy the company of others. My brother is consistently one of the last ones to finish eating. It is generally the three of us kids who do the dishes. The parents have prepped the meal, so it is only fair. As each person finishes we pass our fondue forks on to someone else that hasn't finished as it expedites their cooking. After the dishes are done, we will pass out presents, and until recently we've read the Christmas story. I think we've given it up as I think we know it pretty well by now.

We will then take turns opening presents. Each person opens one before it is the next person's turn. We go around the circle until they are all opened. We used to buy for everyone and then a couple of years ago I suggested we draw names with a dollar cap. It's a lot simpler and cost effective. Even though I don't have to, I usually will still get a small something for my parents and Carol (who is an exceedingly special family friend). Her tie to our family goes back over sixty years.

For years, the only reason I went to services on Christmas Eve was to see Carol. Since she started spending her Christmas with us, I no longer attend church at all. So after we've eaten and opened presents, the others will go to Church and I will head for home.

There you have it, kid.

Talk later.

Roses in the Basement

Tammy Katz
Minnesota

When I was a kid, we always got the Sunday paper. When times were good, we got the daily paper, but we always got the Sunday Paper. My dad would stretch out the Sunday 'funnies" in his big bricklayer arms and I would sit on his lap behind the screen of the funnies while we read and giggled.

After the newspaper was properly read, it was a one way street for that paper; out of the house. There were two ways out, either used in the fireplace to start a fire or stacked and tied neatly with twine into bundles for recycling.

When that one way street reversed, I knew it was a special day. The paper came into the house, down the basement stairs and landed on my dad's work bench. The work bench had all kinds of precious and magical tools I was not allowed to touch because they were too sharp or dangerous, but oftentimes I spent hours looking at them and marveling at my dad's talent at using them and turning out beautifully made wood projects. There were also many, many Miracle Whip jars with their lids nailed to the underside of the shelf where they were filled up with nails, screws and other handyman things, and screwed up to rim to "hang" for easy viewing.

On the special days, when the newspaper came back in, all the tools were covered up by it and the treasures in the jars ignored, for after the work bench was swathed with newspapers, out came the deep fryer and the rosette irons.

A silent cheer would rise in my chest, because I knew now I would get to spend the whole day making rosettes with my dad. Dad and I were not allowed to make rosettes in the kitchen as the deep fryer's soil popped and spit and made a huge mess that my mom was NOT going to clean up. But at my dad's basement workbench, the mess didn't bother him as most of it landed on the newspaper which we rolled up and put back on the one way street to the fireplace when we finished.

We carried down the big mixing bowl and ingredients from the kitchen and mixed up the batter which always seemed too runny to amount to much. My Dad would screw the pretty snowflake-shaped rosette irons to their handles and after covering a cooling area with waxed paper, we got busy with dipping the irons into the batter just so deep, and then holding them in the oil until they dropped off and turned golden brown. Then my dad would carefully scoop them up and put them on the waxed paper to cool. I remember his big bricklayers "mitts" on mine, holding the irons over the oil and protecting my tender hand from the oil splashes. Nothing could get through that tough bricklayer skin and nothing was gonna hurt me if my dad had anything to say about it.

219

For hours, it seemed, we made rosettes and then we meticulously covered them with a light but even coating of powdered sugar and then packed them into department store gift boxes we saved from last year's Christmas presents. Only two layers per box, separated by wax paper of course, we didn't pile them any higher for fear our beautiful snowflake creations would crumble under the weight of the others on top.

Of course, we always ate a few (too many) and there were always the "mistake" or two that had to "be taken care of."

The next best thing to spending the day making rosettes with my dad was giving them to others. A box for my Grandma Na-na, a box for my Grandma Betty, and so on. Each recipient exclaimed over the beauty and precision of each rosette; that's how my dad, the perfectionist, made them. His precise technique never made me nervous or worried, it was just the way we did it. He was confident and patient and on a cold winter day in Minnesota, making snowflake rosettes is one of the best memories my dad ever gave me.

RECIPES

 ere I add recipes for the day: both traditional and from a different country/culture. I hope that you will try a few of these recipes and perhaps incorporate them into your family traditions.

Lefse

My best friend in the whole world, I guess my BFF in Brooklyn, (go Stacey!) (LOL) would spend some Sunday afternoons at her house making Lefse and eating them with tons of butter and brown sugar. Lefse are easy to make and keep well.

Ingredients

- 6 medium-sized potatoes

- 1/3 cup shortening like Crisco or margarine

- 3 tbsp. butter

- 2 tsp. salt (I used one)

- 1/3 cup cream

- 3 cups flour

Directions

Cook the potatoes until well done. Mash together with the butter, lard, salt and cream. Mix ingredients together until smooth.

When the mashed potatoes are cool, add the flour and mix with your hands. Add more flour if the dough is too sticky, and add more cream if the dough is too stiff.

Roll into a long log about three inches in diameter. Place into the refrigerator for about an hour to chill.

Remove from the refrigerator and cut into equal segments, about an inch thick. Roll out on a well floured surface with a rolling pin until less than ¼ inch thick. Place onto the well-oiled griddle and brown on both sides. Using a spatula or a special "lefse stick" (I didn't buy one, I muddled about until I managed with my spatula), remove it from the the griddle and place it on a paper towel lined plate. You can generally stack them five high and then place another paper towel to separate them. We used to butter them and then spread brown sugar on them and roll them up.

Leissi Katten - Kitty Rolls

Ok, I tried. I really did. There was this recipe for Leissi Katter rolls, which means Little Kitty rolls in Swedish, I think. In any case, they are sweet rolls shaped like kitties with raisins for eyes and flavored with saffron. The saffron also gives it a nice yellow color, which is a one of the traditional ways of honoring the sun. Yellow color equals sun, get it? Meanwhile, I will share a quick and easy recipe for a version of Leissi Katter that you can make. It won't be as yellow, but hey, the thought was there!!!

My Version of Leissi Katten:

Ingredients

- 1 package of cinnamon rolls

- 1/4 cup raisins

- cat cookie cutter

Directions

Open the tube of cinnamon rolls. Using a rolling pin, flatten each roll out enough so as to fit the cookie cutter of your choice once, if not twice. Place raisins in eye locations. Cook as instructed on the package. When SLIGHTLY cooled, frost with the glaze, which, coincidentally, is yellow. (Homage to the Sun) Tada!

Snowball Dumplings

There is a dumpling theme going on here. What can I say? They are round and white, it works with the whole Snow Day theme. Work with me. ☺

Ingredients

- 2 cups rice flour

- ¼ tsp. salt

- ¼ cup packed brown sugar

- ¾ cup plus 3 Tbsp. canned unsweetened coconut milk

- 1 cup coconut

- 1 tsp. vanilla

Directions

Stir together rice flour, coconut milk, vanilla and salt in a bowl until a thick paste forms. With floured hands roll into a small ball, about two inches or so wide. Make a small dent in the dough with your thumb. Place a small teaspoon of brown sugar in the dent and enclose the sugar with the dough. Roll dough in extra flour to coat the dumpling and lay it on a wax paper covered plate.

Bring a pot of water to boil and drop dumplings in, about five pieces at a time. Stir gently to prevent them merging into one large dumpling. Cook until the filling has melted, about 10–15 minutes. Again, like most dumplings, they will float to the top when done. But double check and cut one open to make sure the sugar has melted.

Remove from the boiling water with a slotted spoon and place on a paper towel to drain. While still warm, roll in coconut to coat the dumpling. Let it cool completely before serving.

Pumpkin Cheesecake

My older sister Heather makes this fantabulous Pumpkin Cheesecake. I don't like pumpkin pie, pumpkin bread, pumpkin ice cream, and the thought of Harry Potter's pumpkin juice makes me gag!! This cheesecake, however, could convert me.

Ingredients

- 3 packages Cream cheese, softened

- 3 eggs

- 1 can (15 oz) pumpkin pie filling

- 1 cup white sugar

- ½ cup brown sugar
- 2/3 cup condensed milk
- 1 ½ tsp. cornstarch
- ½ tsp. cinnamon
- ¼ tsp. nutmeg
- 2 10" Graham cracker crumb pie shells

Topping:

- 12 oz. Sour Cream
- ¼ cup white sugar
- ¼ tsp. Vanilla

Glaze:

- 1 cup Powdered Sugar
- 2 tsp. of orange juice

Directions

Mix the cream cheese until it becomes creamy, then incorporate the eggs and continue to blend. Next, add condensed milk and pumpkin, and blend thoroughly. Combine all of the dry ingredients and mix them in as well. Pour the resulting batter into the pie shells, filling them until about an inch from the top. For added moisture, place a shallow pan of water on the bottom oven shelf. Bake at 300°F for 30–40 minutes or until the mixture sets. Lastly, prepare the sour cream topping, pour it over the pie, and bake for an additional 5 minutes.

PUZZLES

```
S E M I T L A V E I D E M O N M
H J K M F I V E C A N D L E S B
I I O G N L M G N V P A M N O N
M A I D S A M I L K I N G E U F
S A I N T L U C I A I M Y D R U
T T U I O M C D T S W G U E T U
L W H O D G U X S N J T A W C R
T I I R A L V Q C H J Y K S H U
H E A D W R E A T H R F U G E P
T N U O M E H T N O N O M R E S
K G M T C E A L I D Y T U M S Q
K S W O N S D C A J T R R J E A
C T R L U S S E R K A T Z C B E
E I G H T B E A T I T U D E S I
```

Cheese	**Lusser Katz**	**Sermon on the Mount**
Eight Beatitudes	**Maids a Milking**	**Snow**
Five Candles	**Medieval Times**	
Head Wreath	**Saint Lucia**	**Sweden**

CROSS STITCH DESIGN - ST. LUCIA

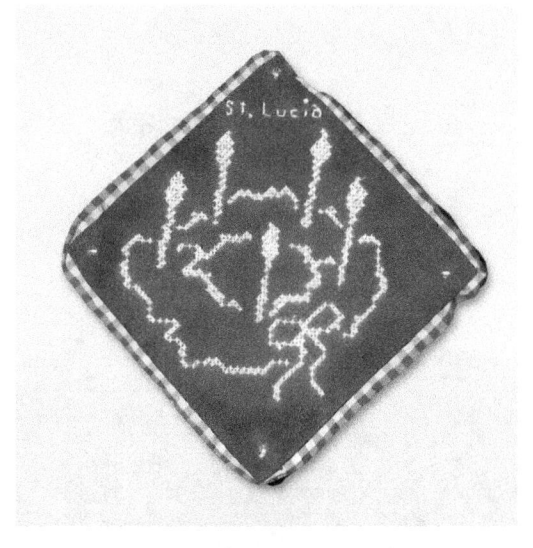

hese are designs for cross stitch patterns that you can use for ornaments, throws or dishcloths. They are a work in progress, so if you can improve upon the design, go for it!!! The patterns might not all be up by Christmas Time, so if the pattern isn't up this week, check back again.

230

COLORING PAGES/RED WORK DESIGN - SANTA LUCIA / SWEDEN

 hese are designs that can be used either for coloring pages for children or copied and transferred to cloth for Redwork for quilts. I kept the lines simple for both those reasons. Many of the designs have dots on them to show where to sew miniature bells or gold beads on them to represent jingle bells.

St. Lucia
Sweden

10 - Italy - Saint Lucia

Long before the Julian Calendar was replaced by the Gregorian Calendar in the 1300s, the longest night/shortest day of the year was December 13th. So in the Scandinavian countries, Yule or Fire Festivals took place on this day. The Latin word for light is lux, lucis, meaning light, daylight. The word Lucifer means Bringer of Light, and the female version of that name is Lucia, so many icons of the Winter Solstice will have a form of that Latin word in their name somewhere. The Goths—forerunners to the Vikings—brought this tale of a Maiden of Light to Southern and Central Europe.

In Sweden, this day is the unofficial beginning of the Christmas Season. The Legend of Saint Lucia or St. Lucy, has numerous origins. One begins like this: Long ago in the depths of winter, Sweden was on the verge of mass starvation. Out of Lake Vaettern, rays of light began appearing on the horizon. From the darkness emerged a longship, heavily laden with foodstuffs and grain. At the helm was a beautiful maiden with long flowing golden hair, dressed in white with a red sash. With her arrival, the people were saved.

In the darkness of the early morning on December 13th, the eldest daughter in the household dons a white robe to symbolize snow and a red sash to symbolize light and re-birth. On her head, she wears a wreath of lingonberry berry leaves, also a symbol of the returning light. She carries a tray of Lusserkatter or cat shaped saffron flavored buns with raisins for eyes, and pepparkakkor or ginger snaps, and coffee as refreshments to wake up the family to prepare for the Festivities.

Today, the Lucia Bride has Handmaidens and Star Boys to assist her with this ritual. Some towns elect a "Lucia" to lead a procession to Church services, followed by singing and a buffet.

NINE LADIES DANCING

In mid-winter farmers lit bonfires and held round dances, celebrating the harvest and looking forward to the spring. The ashes went into the fields for the spring planting. The dancers, usually women, always moved to the left, mimicking the sun's movement from east to west.

In mid-winter, the farmers lit bonfires and held dances in the round, celebrating the Harvest and looking forward to the Spring. The ashes went into the fields for the Spring planting. The dancers, usually women, always moved to the left (also known as widdershins) mimicking the Sun's movement from East to West. The Latin word for left is *Sinistre*, (the root word for sinister), and the direction of left is associated with women, whereas the right side of things is associated with the male.

I read a saying on the internet that I cannot correctly place right now but when I read it, I absolutely loved it, the phrasing was just so beautifully done. It read, "They beat their feet to wake the Earth" in reference to the women dancing in honor of the Spring planting and for the promise of a good yield at Harvest. Isn't that the nicest thought? Waking the earth with the thrumming of your feet.

Also known as Evergreen Day

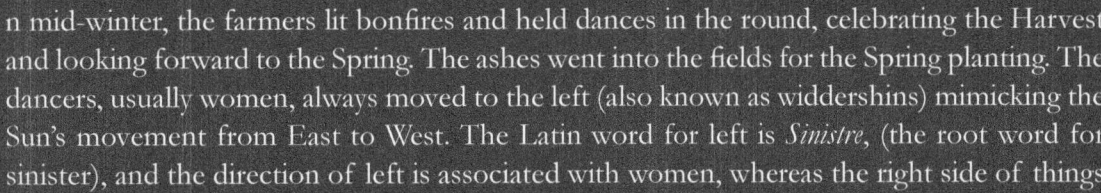

236

BIBLICAL INTERPRETATION

The Nine Ladies Dancing symbolize the nine fruits of the Holy Spirit: Love-charity, joy, peace, patience, gentleness, goodness, faith, meekness and temperance.

 he Nine Ladies Dancing symbolize the Nine Fruits of the Holy Spirit: Love, Charity, Joy, Peace, Patience, Gentleness, Goodness, Faith, Meekness, and Temperance.

238

ANOTHER CULTURE'S WINTER CELEBRATION

Ramadan   Islam
Sep 24-Oct 24 2006

Ramadan and Eid ul Fitr

Muslims have numerous holidays around the calendar year. They have a lunar calendar which means their holidays are always moving. In 2002 and 2003, they were close to the time of Solstice and Christmas and other Festivals of Light, but as the years went by, they moved slowly backwards. In 2010, Ramadan began on August 11th and finished on September 11th. Ramadan is not a festival of actual light but of spiritual light. It is a month-long period of fasting from morning til night. It is done as an act of faith to show purity in one's life, so as to help remind people of the blessings in their lives. They cannot eat or drink anything during the daytime hours, nothing until sundown.

Ramadan ends with another Festival called Eid ul Fitr. There are four Eids throughout the Muslim calendar year. Eid means happiness. Eid is a four-day celebration of the end of Ramadan. It is not only a celebration of the end of the fast, but it is a time to thank God for helping them be strong and practice self-control. Eid ul Fitr is four days of families visiting one another, parties and gatherings, picnics and outings in the cities. Huge banquets to end the Fast are held and the food is unbelievable!! One of the treats made at this time is Mamool, or traveler cookies, a soft semolina flour cookie with date or pistachio filling. There is another treat, honeyed dates, that I had while I was in Iraq that the guards brought back with them from their homes after Eid. They were roll-your-eyes-back good! I cannot remember what they were called though. Darn it.

Word Knerd

The history of the word Saturday

Latin	Germanic/Norse Gods	Spanish	English
Dies Saturni	Saturn/Saturn's Day	Sabado	Saturday

Books

The Best Eid Ever by Asma Mobin-Uddin
ISBN-978 1590784316

Night of the Moon by Hena Kahn
ISBN-9780811860628

Does my Head Look Big in This By Randa Abdel-Fattah
ISBN-9780439919470

Amahl and the Night Visitors by Gian Carlo Menotti
ISBN-9780688054267b

242

REMEMBRANCES

 hese are the stories I collected from my friends, family, and people I met while traveling overseas, most notably from the Coalition Forces in Camp Bucca, Iraq. These stories are their most favorite memories of their Winter Celebrations and Traditions.

Abid with the Blue Eyes

Iraqi Guard, Compound 16
Camp Bucca, Iraq

When I was four years old, my brothers and my father gave me gifts, especially in the East and celebrated with my family members. and I remember I went with my friends to the park to enjoy and get pleasure. All the time we spent in the park, and came back before night, and have traditional habits like giving us money to buy sweets and chocolate, but I like just one thing my mother told about surprises like hiding something behind her back and suddenly to tell me "I have gifts for you." So this thing has affected my heart forever, so I cannot forget those things and all these times repeat in my memory and my heart.

Currently, I am overwhelmed by a deep sense of sadness, primarily because I no longer have my mother, and my father departed from our lives four years ago. I bring up these hardships to illustrate the stark contrast between my life with my mother and the one I lead without her. I believe that once I am married, my circumstances will improve.

Sabah

Compound 16
Camp Bucea, Iraq

In the beginning of this subject, I would like to let you know that there are two Eids in one year for the Muslims. The most important one is Eid al-Fitr. In this Eid, the Muslims break the fast after Ramadan. After they pass the test of Ramadan by being patient and pure of Belief in Allah, they will be rewarded by Allah. That's why Muslims are so happy with this Eid. We also visit families and relatives, going from house to house. We also raise money to aid the poor, because that pleases Allah. The second Eid is Eid al-Adha. This Eid comes after the Haj, the annual Pilgrimage to Mecca.

On the morning of this Eid, we go to visit our relatives' graves to remember them and to grieve for them, as they will always be with us in our memories.

Then we cut the animals I sacrifice to Allah. Then we go and have a huge picnic with the family. The second day of this Eid (there are four days in this Eid), I go with my friends to have fun around the town, in spite of the difficulties in Iraq at this time. That's why we pray to Allah to bless us with health and security. I am grateful to you for this opportunity to open my heart and talk about a part of my life and how we receive these special occasions. I wish you all the best of luck and success in this life, and I apologize if I talk too much.

Day 9

RECIPES

ere I add recipes for the day: both traditional and from a different country/culture. I hope that you will try a few of these recipes and perhaps incorporate them into your family traditions.

Traveler's Cookies/Mamool (this recipe takes two days)

Following the Holiday of Ramadan, there is Eid ul Fitr, which is the celebration of the end of Ramadan. During this time, there is a lot of feasting and family parties. One of the sweets favored at this time is a cookie called Maamool, or Travelers Cookies. I found this recipe on www.Gourmet-Sleuth.com. You can also buy the cookie molds for the recipe at this website or you can go google the closest Middle Eastern grocery in your neighborhood. Google Al Madina grocery. That's where I bought my wooden cookie mold.

There are several different types; each has a design inside to make an imprint on the cookie so as to tell the buyer what sort of filling is inside. The two I saw were pistachios and date filling. Call the grocery at 919-755-6220 and ask the clerk if they have a store near you. I made the cookies from the recipe below and it was a tad too mealy for me so I cut the semolina flour in half with regular flour and it held together better. You try it and decide.

Ingredients

- ½ cup solid shortening

- 8 Tbsp. butter

- 1 cup flour, all purpose

- ¼ tsp. salt

- ¼ tsp. baking powder

- ¼ cup granulated sugar

- 7 Tbsp. water

- 2 cups semolina

Directions

Melt shortening and butter together, or use all butter if you want a richer cookie. Cool slightly. Mix the flour, semolina, salt, baking powder, and sugar together. Rub the shortening into the flour mixture with your fingers until it is a soft, fine meal. Cover the bowl and let it rest overnight.

The next day, sprinkle the seven tablespoons of water over the dough ball and knead it well. Dust the Maamool molds well with flour. Tap out the excess flour. Make a ball of dough, eyeball it to make sure it is enough to fill the mold, and then flatten it out slightly. Place a tsp. of filling into the indentation and close the dough around the filling, and roll it around to seal it in. Place the dough ball into the mold and press lightly. Level off the cookie with the lip of the mold. Be sure the filling isn't showing or it will stick to the pan.

Tap cookies out onto the work area with a sharp, firm hit to the top of the mold. Transfer cookies to the baking sheet with a spatula. Put in the fridge overnight; so molded cookies bake better after "settling up" overnight. Bake at 300 to 325°F for about 10–12 minutes, until barely colored. Cool. Sprinkle or rub with confectioners sugar before serving.

Filling:

- 1½ cups chopped dates
- 6 Tbsp. butter

Directions

Cook dates with butter over medium heat. Mash and stir until completely pureed. Let it cool before filling the cookies.

Passover Cookies

I didn't make these cookies but NOT because I didn't want to. I flat out couldn't find a Matzo meal. I went to Trader Joe's, all the local Grocery stores and Whole Foods. Nuttin! I even tried to ask a rabbi or two at two local Synagogues. No response. I even tried to google a location online, nada.

But I had to put this recipe out there. It sounded too good, and as soon as I find some Matzo meal... I am making them. Chocolate is good in anything!!!!

Ingredients

- ½ stick of butter

- ¾ cup light brown sugar

- 2 large egg yolks

- 1 tsp. vanilla

- 8 oz. Bittersweet chocolate, melted

- ¼ cup matzo meal

- ¼ tsp. salt

- 4 large eggs

- 8 oz. semi sweet chips

Directions

Preheat the oven to 350°F.

Beat butter, sugar, yolks, and vanilla until fluffy. Add Matzo meal and salt. Add melted bittersweet chocolate. Beat egg whites until stiff peaks form. Gently fold into the chocolate mixture and stir. Add chips. Let it stand for 15 minutes. Scoop two-inch balls onto parchment lined paper. Bake for 10–12 minutes. Cool for 10 minutes.

Jello Cookies

I love these things!!! You can change the color and the flavor as many times as there are flavors and colors of Jello. Think of a Holiday and you can probably match it up with a color.

Anyhoo…

Ingredients

- ¾ cup shortening, like Crisco

- ½ cup granulated sugar

- 1 small box of Jello (any flavor)

- 2 eggs

- 1 tsp. vanilla

- 2 ½ cups all purpose flour

- 1 tsp. salt

- 1 tsp. baking powder

- 1 cup granulated sugar

Directions

In a large bowl, cream together the Crisco and a half cup of sugar using an electric mixer. Add eggs, vanilla and jello. Mix well. Stir in flour, baking powder and salt. Shape into 1-inch balls. Place on greased cookie sheets and flatten with a water glass dipped into a cup of sugar. Bake for 8-10 minutes. Enjoy.

PUZZLES

They beat their feet to wake the Earth

```
N A P E P F B A Q E U E V O L N M A L S I A B T Z
F R U I T S O F T H E H O L Y S P I R I T X N G P
S Q C P T Q N P N A L U R O U N D D A N C E S L E
E T R Q N A S P R I N G P L A N T I N G M T N S E
X C N S E H S A E A A I Y I I B Q M E N U A E G P
H N A C K V E L N C A B Y O Q R X J E D D H N G E
X O Y E H F A B P O T U W T D B P T O Y E I E H N
I Y L E P I E C P T A L Z G B U H H F Y C N R E R
A G R L M O D Q J I P J U R F G U D Y N T O E X U
L A M A Y O D U U K M P P D I A Q L A L E R K U I
S R O J V E I S M O U J U L O U E D E Z G D P W B
N E J Q A S H D D C V I N M G C S N C R D E T Q Z
D V B S U Y I O L P I E O T N E E H E G C A M M E
G N I R J S E U L C L Y H A I S A V F B E Z C A W
T A T O Y S J O P A U R R D S R E Y O Z I U W P Y
H D N K F B J W U D H E A F I B D N T L I J M M X
D A T U X A Y T S R P L J T M S F O S I F N B Y I
Y M P U W Y I E R M I C Y R D I Z E P J R G P R A
E A Z M T R E I E I S J J Q R A V E O B M U O S V
P R F B I W I T E U F Y D E F E C N E I T A P S X
D R K P S S E V K N N M S S S E N K E E M A O M S
I L S I Q S O R Y F H O D R U T T F I V F D R S L
```

Ashes	**Charity**	**Round**	**Patience**
Islam	**Joy**	**Dances**	**Temperance**
Peace	**Ramadan**	**Fruits of the Holy Spirit**	
Bonfires	**Evergreen**	**Love**	
Ivy	**Ladies**	**Spring Planting**	
Purity	**Dancing**	**Holly**	

CROSS STITCH DESIGN - MUSLIM CRESCENT MOON

hese are designs for cross stitch patterns that you can use for ornaments, throws, or dishcloths. They are a work in progress, so if you can improve y upon the design, go for it! The patterns might not all be up by Christmas Time, so if the pattern isn't up this week, check back again.

India

Bada Din - Big Day

3 - India - Babba/Bada Din

About 2.3 percent of the people of India are Christians, about twenty-four million people. Their version of Santa is called Babba and Christmas Day is known as Bada Din or "Big Day". Each province celebrates Christmas differently. They decorate banana or mango trees with ornaments and tinsel and brightly colored lights. They also light small oil-burning lamps as Christmas decorations and fill their churches with red flowers. They give presents to family members and baksheesh, or charity, to the poor people.

In India, the poinsettia is in flower during Christmas, so many objects use the star-shape of the poinsettia in their design, such as clay oil lamps and tree ornaments. Many churches are decorated with this brilliant bloom for the Christmas Midnight Mass.

In Southern India, Christians put small clay lamps on the rooftops and walls of their houses at Christmas, a carryover of the tradition of welcoming the new Dawn, just as the Hindus do during their festival called Diwali. It is traditional to stay up all night with family, singing and dancing, eating special treats, waiting to be the first to welcome the new day as the sun rises.

256

COLORING PAGES/RED WORK DESIGN-ARABIAN SANTA/UNITED ARAB EMIRATES

hese are designs that can be used either for coloring pages for children or copied and transferred to cloth for Redwork for quilts. I kept the lines simple for both those reasons. Many of the designs have dots on them to show where to sew miniature bells or gold beads on them to represent jingle bells.

TEN LORDS A-LEAPING

Leaping dances were usually done by men-danced for good luck in fertility and war. The Lord's a-leaping come from the Morris dancers which are descended from the Moorish dancers: The moors were the African people who occupied northwest Africa, or present day morocco and Mauritania.

The Lord's A-Leaping comes from the Morris dancers of old England and they are in turn descended from the Moorish dancers. The leaping dances were done strictly by men in preparation for War and Harvest time. The Moors were the African people who occupied Northwest Africa or present day Morocco and Mauritania. Leaping dances were usually done by men—danced for good luck in fertility and war. The Roman God of Vegetation and War (what a mix!?!) was Mars. The Romans and the Moorish dancers believed that the corn would grow as high as the highest leaps made by the male dancers. Swords were always part of the costume.

Also known as St. Distaff's Day.

There is actually no Saint Distaff. I really think at this point in the song and the naming of the days and the festivities, that whoever was assigning days just ran out of ideas and gave over the day to the hard working weavers of the day. Lord knows the working man could have used an additional day off. A distaff is the rod upon which the fibers are spun during the weaving process.

Women of all classes spun fibers in whatever spare time they had. Before the invention of the spinning wheel, spinning was done on the distaff. It was long and hard work, one pound of spun wool could take about a week to spin. Unmarried women had more time on their hands than married women so they did more spinning.

Here comes another **Word Knerd**: Unmarried women then became known as spinsters. The distaff is also a symbol of Women, due to its domestic nature. The distaff side and the spear side were legal terms in France, distaff being for women and spear for men. A French proverb reads "The crown of France never falls to the distaff".

Unfortunately, and also, typically, women went back to work after the Holidays before the men. Women would go back to the day-to-day grind on St. Distaff's Day whereas men could wait til Plough Monday, when ploughs were officially blessed for the coming year. Slackers. A popular rhyme from a book of poems called "Hesperides" reads:

Partly work and partly play
Yon must work on St. Distaff's Day
From the plow soon free your team
Then come home and father them
If the maids a-spinning go
Burn the flax and burn the tow
Bring in pails of water then
Let the maids bewash the men
Give St. Distaff all the right
Then bid Christmas sport good night
And next morrow every one
To his own vocation

Apparently, even as the women had to go back to work before the men, the men got to make sport of them and tease them by harassing them, setting their wool on fire and generally bugging them. The women could retaliate by throwing buckets of water on the men. Yay girls!!!

BIBLICAL INTERPRETATION

The Ten Lords
A-Leaping
symbolize the Ten
Commandments.

he Ten Lords A-Leaping symbolize the Ten Commandments.

262

Day 10

ANOTHER CULTURE'S WINTER CELEBRATION

Hanukah Dec 15-23

Hanukkah

What of Hanukkah, the Jewish Festival of Lights that occurs around this time every year? Is it related to other celebrations of the season?

The placement of Hanukkah is tied to both the lunar and solar calendars. It begins on the 25th of Kislev, three days before the new moon closest to the Winter Solstice. It commemorates an historic event—the Maccabees' victory over the Greeks and the rededication of the temple at Jerusalem. According to legend, when the day of rededication came, only enough oil for one day could be found. But that small amount miraculously burned for eight days. The modern-day celebration revolves around the lighting of the candles on the Menorah.

The menorah has eight candle holders with another place to hold the extra candle used to light the others. A blessing is said each night as the candles are lit and children receive small gifts each night, dreidels (spinning tops), Hanukkah Gelt (money), or chocolate coins. The food most famous for this holiday are Latkes, potato pancakes, and Sufgiyot, jelly filled doughnuts. The principal source for the story of Hanukkah is the Talmud.

But the form of this celebration, a Festival of Lights (with candles at the heart of the ritual), makes Hanukkah wonderfully compatible with other celebrations at this time of year. As a symbolic celebration of growing light and as a commemoration of spiritual rebirth, it also seems closely related to other observances.

As with the Native Americans who became Christians, some Jewish people wanted a Santa figure of their own. You can thank Adam Sandler for that, folks, not me, and oh yeah. Saturday Night Live. Together, they created Hanukkah Harry, who delivers toys and treats to good little Jewish boys and girls during Hanukkah while being pulled on a cart drawn by three donkeys. The donkeys are named Moishe, Hershel and Schlomo. There's a song too, but you can go to Youtube for that one. It's pretty funny. Totally DID NOT make this up. But, I did have to draw a picture of it. Had to. It came out pretty good too. ☺

Word Knerd

The history of the word Sunday

Latin	Germanic/Norse Gods	Spanish	English
Dies Solis/Domini	Sonntag or Sun Day	Domingo	Sunday
Day of the Sun			

Books

Hershel and the Hanukkah Goblins by Eric Kimmel
ISBN-9780823411313

Matzo Ball Moon by by Leslea Newman
ISBN-9780618604814

Maccabee! The Story of Hanukkah by Tilda Balsley
ISBN-9780761345084

266

REMEMBRANCES

hese are the stories I collected from my friends, family and people I met while traveling overseas, most notably from the Coalition Forces in Camp Bucca, Iraq. These stories are their most favorite memories of their Winter Celebrations and Traditions.

Becoming a Man?

Evy and Richard S.
Windsor, Vt.

Anyway, I've been bugging my husband for a Holiday story and he won't cooperate! He just told me about a Passover celebration when he was thirteen. How they would read passages from the Bible about the Exodus, when Jews were led by Moses. They state the Twelve Plagues of Egypt, that the Pharaoh imposed on Jews to quell their attempts to leave Egypt and their lives as slaves. Each time a statement is read, everyone takes a sip of wine from their glasses and gives thanks to God for rescuing them from that particular plague. Richard, thirteen at the time, followed their lead and sipped wine until his glass was empty. An Uncle refilled his glass (probably when his parents weren't looking) and Richard, being only thirteen, polished it off quickly.

In the middle of the Passover meal, the alcohol took its effect on Richard to the point where he had to excuse himself for feeling sick. As soon as his head hit the pillow, he passed out. Not only did he miss the rest of the Passover meal, but he woke up with a pounding headache and not only that, but then he had to face the wrath of his parents!!!

Ryan O.
Controller, Compound 16
NPDB4
Camp Bucca, Iraq

So I am in the desert of Iraq, a good place for a Jew, right? My friend Tammy asked me to write her a story about my favorite holiday growing up. Being the only Jew in my Unit I was touched. That was a nice way of saying thanks but no thanks. So, after being in the desert for several months and a ten dollar bet with her later (that I won), here is my story.

First you have to understand my family. We are like most American families except my dad is from New Zealand and my mom is from Miami. My dad converted to Judaism for my mom (way to stand up, dad), so there are several things my dad does badly: one is speak Hebrew, two is read Hebrew and three is get tipsy off of wine. Then there are my sisters. I have a twin sister named Heather and an older but not wiser sister Karen. Both love to gang up on me and my dad and tell us the glory of womanhood and how men suck. My mom is my mom; what can I say? Like most Jewish moms, she tells me I never call home enough and asks how things are at least three times every ten minutes.

How does this relate to my favorite holiday? Well, when I think of my favorite holiday, I think of Passover, or Pesach in Hebrew. I think of my family. It is my favorite because all the family gets together and you can eat all you want, celebrating. Jews freedom from slavery. So at Passover, there's no table rules. You want a pillow you bring a pillow; you want a toy, you bring a toy to the table. For a kid, that is the best thing ever. This is called the Passover Seder.

During the Seder, my Dad tells the story of Passover and there are several parts to it. During the different parts, you eat different things. Like bitter herbs to symbolize the bitterness of slavery. You also set out a glass of wine and candles for the Prophet Eliyahu.

My dad always led the Seder with bad Hebrew and a glass of wine. My dad would read the Haggadah or the story of Passover. My mom would try to keep him on track by whispering the correct words, or how to say them correctly. When my dad would get frustrated, he would say "another prayer of the wine" and we would all laugh. It was always funny to see my dad stumble through Hebrew, like a kid trying to ride a bike. Then there's the food, after the Passover Ceremony. My mom always made an awesome dinner. Matzah ball soup to start, which one likes ok, but the latkes (potato pancakes) my mom makes are the best. They always go fast in my house. Then there is the brisket. Need I say more? After dinner, my sisters and I go find the Afikomen, which are pieces of Matzah or special bread that my dad hid from us. We find it, give it to our parents and they give us a present.

Then, after dinner, we all clean up, sing Hebrew songs like Dahyenu (It would have been enough for us) and Eliyahu Ha-Navi (Elijah the Prophet). My dad would always drink the glass of wine off the table and then say "Look, Eliyahu drank it". Worked until I was five years old, but he still does it every year. So that's my Holiday memory and now Tammy owes me ten bucks and you know all about my crazy family.

270

RECIPES

 ere I add recipes for the day: both traditional and from a different country/culture. I hope that you will try a few of these recipes and perhaps incorporate them into your family traditions.

Carolina Cornbread

This isn't really cornbread. But it does have a really cool story with it. My friends and I like to go to an antique store down in Selma, called The Mill.

Inside, there are about thirty cats walking, sleeping and purring around. Numerous pooches and puppies too, all looking for homes. This is a very cool store, with a unique Proprietress by the name of Miss Raylene. You can call her up and ask her for an item and out of the hundreds of thousands of items in her store (which is, in fact, a real old Mill from the 1800s) she can pin point it and have it waiting for you when you arrive.

Anyways, in the center of this store is a nice little old lady with a small hotdog stand. Her name is Miss Betty. She was manning the hot dog stand one hot day and I wandered by and saw a baked good item that rather looked like a Blondie. I was a wee bit peckish, so I asked about it and she called it a bit of Carolina Cornbread. She explained it wasn't cornbread but rather a sort of Blondie with chopped Pecans. Not a huge fan of nuts or cornbread but, like I said, I was hungry so I bought one. It was the best brownie/blondie/nut thing/whatever I had ever eaten. It was sugar sublime!! So I asked Miss Betty to share the recipe with me and she promised to mail the recipe when she got a moment.

Two weeks later, she did just that, and I hopped on it like white on rice. My first effort was so heavy, I feared to drop it and risk my toes. Too much oil, but I had followed the recipe to a Tea. What went wrong? So, the next one, I lost the oil and of course, it was too dry.

So there began the tweaking and adjusting of the recipe. Finally, after four batches and subjecting my co-workers to numerous attempts, I came up with a really decadent and luscious and unbelievably yummy Carolina Cornbread recipe. Even if you don't like nuts, give it a try, and if you are ever in Selma, North Carolina, do a drive-by of The Mill and stop in. Walk in and pet the animals, say hey to Miss Raylene and search for Miss Betty. You won't be sorry.

Ingredients

- 1½ cups flour

- 1¼ cups finely crushed Pecans

- 2 eggs

- ½ tsp. vanilla

- 1 cup brown sugar

- 1 cup white sugar

- 2 tsp. vanilla

- ½ tsp. cinnamon

- 1/3 cup oil

- ½ cup Chunky Applesauce

Use a two inch Jelly roll pan, or spread the batter thinly in a normal pan. It bakes better as a thin bar rather than a thick one)

Directions

Preheat the oven to 350°F.

Mix dry ingredients together first. Beat the eggs in a separate bowl, add the oil and applesauce. Gradually add the dry ingredients to the wet. Mix well. Spread batter in the Jelly Roll pan. Bake for 15–18 minutes or until the top is nicely browned. Let cool, cut, separate, and serve!!

Ice Cream Cake Dessert

This is my mom and Aunt's go-to summer dessert. Very easy and extremely versatile, you can change the liquor used to suit your tastes.

Ingredients

- 1 pack of Ice Cream Sandwiches (12 pcs.)

- 1 pack Heath Bar bits

- 1 8 oz. container of Cool Whip

- 12 Tbsp. Kahlua

Directions

Sprinkle 8 tablespoons of Kahlua on the bottom of the pan. Unwrap Ice Cream bars and lay at the bottom of the pan. Mix Cool Whip with the remaining Kahlua and spread over bars. Sprinkle with Heath Bar bits. Cover and freeze.

Latkes

Ingredients

- 1½ cups grated raw potatoes
- 1 cup all purpose flour
- 1 cup leftover mashed potatoes
- 1 egg
- salt and pepper
- 1/4 cup olive oil

Directions

In a bowl, mix the grated potatoes and flour. Blend in the mashed potatoes.

In another bowl, whisk together the egg, the milk, and seasonings. Mix in with the potato mixture. Pat into little patties about 4 inches across.

Heat olive oil in a large skillet over medium heat. Drop in patties and fry until golden brown. Drain on a paper towel lined plate. Serve warm with sour cream or applesauce.

276

PUZZLES

```
M O R R I S D A N C E R S R F V
F E R T I L I T Y W A R T F R O
G N I P A E L A S D R O L F W S
S E C N A D G N I P A E L A U I
T E N C O M M A N D M E N T S E
M O R R I S H D A N C E R S I H
Z E A C I X H P F T E S H I A A
U I S N M C U O R D C P M D M N
A E P A E F E N Y I T I I T D U
D R E I D E L S E T E N Z N Q K
A F R I C A M R Y N A N T I P K
E O O A M R E A N T N I B A N A
L H E U G B D G V A U N L S M H
I M J D W T G O S E J G O P C A
```

Africa	**Fertility**	**Leaping Dances**
Morris Dancers	**Saint distaff**	**Ten Commandments**
Dreidel	**Hanukkah**	**Lords A-leaping**
Morrish Dancers	**Spinning**	**War**

CROSS STITCH DESIGN - MENORAH

 T hese are designs for cross stitch patterns that you can use for ornaments, throws or dishcloths. They are a work in progress, so if you can improve upon the design, go for it!!! The patterns might not all be up by Christmas Time, so if the pattern isn't up this week, check back again.

Hanukkah Harry
Jewish

8-Jewish-Hanukkah Harry

Hanukkah Harry is a fictional character and first appeared on December 16, 1989 on Saturday Night Live, and was played by Jon Lovitz. He is portrayed as a happy, jolly old man with a beard characteristic of a male adherent of Haredi Judaism, and with his clothes in blue with white edges, which are the colors of the flag of Israel.

The story goes like this:

"It is Christmas Eve and Santa Claus, despite being nursed by Mrs. Claus, is severely ill. Unable to work due to his illness, Santa calls Hanukkah Harry. Hanukkah Harry is a very funny guy who helps out Santa from time to time, and he lives and works in his shop on Mount Sinai. He has a brother named Santa Cohen and his sister's name is Yenta Claus. They have a cousin named Schmanta Claus and they all LOVE Hanukkah.

Mrs. Claus calls and asks Hanukkah Harry if he could fill in to deliver toys to children around the globe. Hanukkah Harry agrees and flies through the air on a cart pulled by three donkeys, Moishe, Hershel and Shlomo. Hanukkah Harry lands on a roof and climbs down the chimney of the home of Scott and Christine, offering gifts of socks and slacks respectively. While the children are initially disappointed at their gifts, their realization that Hanukkah Harry had helped Santa makes them recognize that "Christians and Jews, deep down, are pretty much the same. Maybe that's the true meaning of Christmas!" With that statement, Santa's flu is cured, and Santa comes down the chimney bearing gifts of Barbie make-me-pretty for Christine and a pellet gun for Scott."

As Hanukkah Harry flies through the air, delivering gifts, Sufgiyot (doughnuts) and sizzling hot Latkes to all the good little Jewish boys and girls on the seven nights of Hanukkah, you can hear him call out to his donkeys:

"On Moishe! On Hershel! On Shlomo!
It's Hanukkah Harry 8 nights a year!
On Moishe! On Hershel! On Shlomo!
Means that Hanukkah Harry is here!
Delivering Toys
to Jewish Girls and Jewish Boys
We dance the Horah
Around the Menorah
'cause Hanukkah Harry is here!"

282

ELEVEN PIPERS PIPING

Pipes developed from a single bone or wood flute to bagpipes, adding an animal skin for an airbag They were used at round dances, called caroles. Later, it became an instrument of war because it stirred the soldiers and made them ready for battle.

Pipes developed from a single bone or wood flute to bagpipes, adding an animal skin for an airbag. They were used at Round Dances, called Caroles. Later, it became an instrument of war because it stirred the soldiers and made them ready for battle.

This is also known as the Eve of Epiphany or Twelfth Night.

284

BIBLICAL INTERPRETATION

The Eleven Piper's piping symbolize the eleven faithful disciples: Simon, James the Elder, John the Beloved, Andrew, Philip, Nathanael, Thomas, Matthew, James the Younger, Jude and Simon.

The Eleven Pipers Piping symbolize the eleven faithful disciples: Simon, James the Elder, John the Beloved, Andrew, Philip, Nathanael, Thomas, Matthew, James the Younger, Jude, and Simon.

286

ANOTHER CULTURE'S WINTER CELEBRATION

Twelfth Night - European and American

What of Hanukkah, the Jewish Festival of Lights that occurs around this time every year? Is it related to other celebrations of the season?

Thousands of years ago, there was once this custom that on or about the Winter Solstice, a huge log would be cut down and brought into the house. As long as the log burned, no work could be done. You were celebrating the Yule. Friends and family are to gather, drinking and eating are to take place and of course, gifts are given.

287

Around the 4th Century, during the Nicene Council, it was decided to celebrate the birth of Christ during the Winter Solstice. The Yule log and the celebration of the Light of the Sun became the celebration of the Light of the Son.

There are many additions and stories to the Yule Log tradition. Houses would keep cinders of the previous year's fires to add to the new one. Splinters from the old log were used to kindle the new log. Drink, food, special oils, and prayers written on paper were all placed on the log while it burned, the smoke carrying the prayers to the gods or to Heaven. It was thought that the old year was to be "burned away" with the log, while hopes and prayers for the coming year would be answered by saying prayers and blessings over the log.

In some English manors and in large, rich homes in America, it was a day's event for the whole community to drag the huge log to the house behind a team of horses. In pre-Civil War times, it was said that the slaves wouldn't have to work as long as the Yule log burned. So you know the wisest and most learned men chose the greenest and wettest log they could find! In American Appalachia, the Yule log was called the "backstick" (see more at tomm@mymerrychristmas.com) and like the large well-to-do homes, the log would be so large that it would stick out of the hearth and into the room.

In most cultures, the log would burn from the first day of Christmas, the 26th, to the last on January 6th. January 6th is also the traditionally observed LAST DAY of the Christmas Holiday. At this time, ornaments and greenery were taken down and all trees and boughs taken outside and burned in a bonfire. This was part of the ritualistic cleansing, the "get out the old and bring in the new," the ending of the old year and the looking forward to the new one coming.

But in others, it began several weeks before Solstice and went several weeks after; after all, back in the Medieval Times, really. . .What else was there to do during the winter except to look for food, try to hunt food and keep warm while eating food? In Pagan times, different woods were burned for different religious reasons and different effects:

- Aspen was burned to signify the understanding of the Grand Design.

- Birch signified new beginnings.

- Holly signified visions and past lives.

- Oak signified strength and wisdom.

- Pine signified prosperity.

- Willow signified the Goddess to achieve desires or wishes.

But as time went on and houses became smaller and fireplaces disappeared, the tradition died off. But some tried to keep it going. In France, they turned the Yule Log into the Yule Cake. That tradition thankfully made it over here to America in the form of Jelly Roll cakes! Yum!! Other ways people keep to remember the Yule Log, other than burning it or eating it, is to have a Yule Log candle as a centerpiece on the Holiday Table.

There is yet one more culture/celebration to mention. There will be no Redwork line drawing, or puzzles or recipes for this one as the culture in question is remarkably hard to get ANY information on.

It is the Up Helly Aa Fire Festival celebration in the Shetland Islands. I have written and emailed the Chamber of Commerce in Lerwick, Shetland islands, no less than four times, and never once got any response back. Very little literature on the Fire Festival exists, either on the Net or in hard copy. So what I share with you does come from limited sources. Mainly, from Shetlopedia.com. But it was so fascinating that I had to include it. If you do want to do any designs or coloring about this festival, you can use the Odin/Sleipnir Redwork design if you really want to, as it IS Norse and the Up Helly Aa is Norse in its heritage. But you will have to substitute the mighty steed in the picture with a tiny Shetland pony the Islands are famous for. They don't grow 'em big there.

Anyhoo. A little history about the Islands and then some about the festival itself. About a hundred miles North/Northwest of Scotland and 230 miles West of Norway lies the sub-artic archipelago Shetland Islands. Which means aside from being the Northernmost point of the UK and of Scotland, they are way out in the middle of absolutely-ever-lovin'-NOWHERE. Way, way isolated y'all. (**Point 1**)

The origin of the name "Up Helly Aa" (or Up-Helly-A'), is still a hotly debated point. Generally, though, it is accepted that the term probably refers to a celebration of the last day of Christmas festivities. Historically, the 5th of January was Old Yule, and the 24th day following the 5th was the final day of the Yuletide celebrations—a day of fire and food, mayhem and merrymaking.

To me, it sounds more like a bastardization of the term "Uphaliday", a Lowland Scots term, which refers to the first day after termination of the Christmas holidays. Uphaliday was the popular name for Twelfth Night. (**Point 2**)

(See shetlopedia.com)

The largest island, known simply as the Mainland, has an area of about 375 square miles, making it the third largest Scottish island and the fifth largest of the British Isles. There are about a hundred islands, of which sixteen are inhabited. Lerwick is the largest city and the capital and has a population of around 7,500. The archipelago itself has a total population of about 22,000, half of which live within 10 miles of the town of Lerwick. (**Point 3**)

Shetland has mild winters and short, cool summers. The climate all year round is moderate due to the influence of the surrounding seas, with an average high of 41 °F in March and 57 °F in July. Negative temperatures over seventy degrees are rare. Brrrrr!

A normal day in the Shetlands is cloudy and windy, with an average rainfall of three-fourths of an inch a day, about 250 days a year. (**Point 4**)

Due to the latitude of the islands, the Northern Lights can sometimes be seen in the sky in winter nights, while in summer (all three short months of it) there is almost perpetual daylight, known locally as the "simmer dim".

Human occupation has been dated back to the Mesolithic period, 4320-4030 B.C. and was Norwegian, all the way up until the late 1300s. Jon Haraldsson was the last of an unbroken line of Norse jarls (Norse for Earl), thereafter the earls/jarls were Scots noblemen.

The Up-Helly-Aa Fire Festival

Prior to the 1870s, Yule Festivities in the Shetland Islands were quite violent: bands of drunken men careening about the town, dragging wooden sledges about with burning tar barrels, general mayhem, breaking windows, public drunkenness and smearing tar on buildings. Rather like America fifty years or so prior with the bands of Callithumpians, and rowdy revelers.

Around 1870, a group of young men in the town with intellectual interests injected a series of new ideas into the proceedings. First, they improvised the name Up-Helly-Aa, and gradually postponed the celebrations until the last Tuesday in January. Secondly, they introduced a far more elaborate element of disguise—"guizing" into the new festival. I think men just like dressing up as much as women, if not more!

At the same time, they were toying with the idea of introducing Viking themes to their new festival, paying tribute to their Viking ancestry. In the late 1880s, "da Galley," the Viking Longship, appeared in the proceedings. In the early 1900s, there appeared the "Guizer Jarl," the chief guizer, and it wasn't until after the First World War that there was a squad of Vikings, the "Guizer Jarl's Squad," in the procession every year.

The Up-Helly-Aa event begins early in the morning when the "Da Galley" is escorted to the town pier and ends with a torchlight procession at night. The day is filled with parades, visits to old folks homes and to schools for parties and singing with the children, and smaller events filled with food and dancing. There is also "Da Bill" and this tradition began in the late 1890s. It was a large sign, now a billboard, erected at a central location in the town. It gives general rules and regulations for the Guizers for the day, but it also lists the misdeeds and adventures of town individuals from the preceding year, and pokes fun at authority figures as well.

This is a nod to the Role Reversal themes of the Feast of Fools, Boy Bishop Day, 12th Night King and Queen, etc. Some folks might be offended at being named in the "Da Bill." But over the years, it has become a badge of honor to be mentioned.

The torchlight procession can have hundreds, if not thousands, of people in it. The galley burnings are reminiscent of pagan Norse rituals, where great chieftains were cremated with their treasures. It is widely known and accepted that the traditions and activities of Up-Helly-Aa are not **actual** traditions of Norwegian ancestors handed down but rather a modern-day invention, a nod to the Vikings of yesteryear and a celebration of their impact.

The designs used for the ships and the costumes of the *Guizer Jarls* (Disguised Earls) are generally known as not being authentic and are based on the stereotypes of Vikings and Victorian era romantic ideas rather than on hard facts.

"It's not traditional Viking, it's traditional Up-Helly-Aa," - Anonymous

The Guizers then meet in the evening at a pre-appointed location and are given torches in a certain order. A gun or starter's pistol is fired to signal the beginning of the proceedings. It begins with total darkness, then flares are used to light the torches, and then the torches are held up high. After the light up, the Galley, then the Squads, then a Brass Band of some sort, then the Guizers, all march down to the Pier. They form concentric circles around "Da Galley." Then the Guizer Jarl calls for three cheers

for "da boys dat built da Galley." They then begin to throw torches onto the Longship, front rows first and then on backwards, until all torches have been thrown.

After this, the party begins. There are costume contests, singing demonstrations at various halls, skits, and lots of feasting. The party continues until the early morning hours of the next day. The day following Up-Helly-Aa is a National Holiday. Up-Helly-Aa is also known as Transvestite Tuesday, as the men will dress up in female clothing for the procession, as well as Viking garb.(**Point 5**)

Now, this is a different culture and a different time, but the basic premise is the same. The Five Points from above are all very HUGE reasons why the Fire Festival of the Shetlands exist. Not the only reasons, but they certainly contribute. ☺

Points:

1 - The Islands are VERY isolated.

2 - It is the end of the Yule celebration.

3 - They are a small and isolated population so their manner of celebration is exceptionally unique.

4 - It rains 250 days out of the year, so they would be VERY glad to celebrate the end of winter and welcome in the few days of Sun that they would have.

5 - While both sexes now participate in the procession, it was traditionally a male dominated organization. Being also known as Transvestite Tuesday, it refers to the habit of dressing up as the opposite sex which occurs in almost all Yuletide Festivities worldwide. Examples: Feast of Fools, Mummers and Saturnalia.

The Up-Helly-Aa Song

From grand old Viking centuries Up-Helly-A' has come,
Then light the torch and form the arch, and sound the rolling drum:
And wake the mighty memories of heroes that are dumb;
The waves are rolling on.

Chorus: Grand old Vikings ruled upon the ocean vast,
Their brave battle-songs still thunder on the blast;
Their wild war-cry comes a-ringing from the past;
We answer it "A-oi"!
Roll their glory down the ages,
Sons of warriors and sages,

When the fight for Freedom rages,
Be bold and strong as they!

Of yore, our fiery fathers sped upon the Viking Path;
Of yore, their dreaded dragons braved the ocean in its wrath;
And we, their sons, are reaping now their glory's aftermath;
The waves are rolling on.

Chorus

In distant lands, their raven-flag flew like a blazing star;
And foreign foemen, trembling, heard their battle-cry afar;
And they thundered o'er the quaking earth, those mighty men of war;
The waves are rolling on.

Chorus

On distant seas, their dragon-prows went gleaming outward bound,
The storm-clouds were their banners, and their music ocean's sound;
And we, their sons, go sailing still the wide earth round and round;
The waves are rolling on.

Chorus

No more Thor's lurid Hammer flames against the northern sky;
No more from Odin's shining halls the dark valkyrie fly;
Before the Light the heathen Night went slowly rolling by;
The waves are rolling on.

Chorus

We are the sons of mightly sires, whose souls were staunch and strong;
We sweep upon our serried foes, the hosts of Hate and Wrong;
The glory of a grander Age has fired our battle-song;
The waves are rolling on.

Chorus

Our galley is the People's Right, the dragon of the free;
The Right that rising in its might, brings tyrants to their knee;
The flag that flies above us is the Love of Liberty;
The waves are rolling on.

Words by J. J. Haldane Burgess
Music by Thomas Manson

The Galley Song

Floats the raven banner o'er us,
Round our Dragon Ship we stand,
Voices joined in gladsome chorus,
Raised aloft the flaming brand.

Every guizer has a duty
When he joins the festive throng
Honour, freedom, love and beauty
In the feast, the dance, the song.

Worthy sons of Vikings make us,
Truth be our encircling fire
Shadowy visions backward take us
To the Sea-King's fun'ral pyre.

Bonds of Brotherhood inherit,
O'er strife the curtain draw;
Let our actions breathe the spirit
Of our grand Up-Helly-A'.

Written by John Nicolson, to the tune of an old Norwegian folk song.

The Norseman's Home

The Norseman's home in days gone by
Was on the rolling sea,
And there his pennon did defy
The foe of Normandy.
Then let us ne'er forget the race,
Who bravely fought and died,

Who never filled a craven's grave,
But ruled the foaming tide.
The noble spirits, bold and free

Too narrow was their land,
They roved the wide expansive sea,
And quelled the Norman band.
Then let us all in harmony,
Give honour to the brave
The noble, hardy, northern men,
Who ruled the stormy wave.

**Up-helly-Aa: A century of festival (Hardcover)
by James W Irvine (Author)**

Word Knerd

Christmas Carols

The word carols comes from the Greek word *Choraulein*:

Choros: meaning the dance,

Aulein: means to play the flute.

Before the 1300s, carols were not considered songs at all, but rather dances done in the round. Women would always be in the inner circle and move to the left, mimicking the path of the sun, and men were always on the outer ring, moving to the right. Dances were held at significant times of the year, like at Winter Solstice, to encourage the earth to be fruitful and yield a bountiful harvest in the coming year. Ashes from the fires held at Yule time were saved and plowed into the fields in the spring planting. Dancers at the Carols were encouraged to "beat their feet to wake the earth." The more exuberant the dance, the better the harvest.

The Carols changed over the years from just dances to dances/songs to songs alone. The tradition morphed from one with an Agricultural tone to one of plain frivolity and release. Moving from the countryside to the villages, the singers would go from house to house, singing songs of blessing in exchange for food and drink.

Another tradition in England that came from a borrowed culture was that of the Mummers. Itinerant bands of performers would travel the countryside, stopping at villages and houses of the rich, singing and performing in exchange for food, drink and sometimes, a place to stay. Hundreds of years ago, it was the highlight of the Season to look forward to when the Mummers would come, as their visit would always last several weeks.

That tradition of Mummers/Caroling, people going door to door singing and performing, has continued from European sources to American shores in various forms. Mummers are actually African in origin. The Moors from Morocco began the tradition of traveling entertainment hundreds of years ago when they came to/were brought to the British Isles. The phrase "Moorish dances" morphed into Morris Dancers. Morris Dancers were a major part of any Mummers group and Morris Dancers still perform to this day at village events, fetes and at Renaissance Festivals around the world. Absorbed by numerous cultures, both before and after, the tradition of Mummers arrived in America and continued on in the form of:

Callithumpian bands (New York City), CowBellian Bands (New England), Shivaree (South), Belsnickles (New York), The Wait (Europe), Wassailers and Carolers (USA), and John Canoe Bands (Slave rendition-South). All these modified traditions have the same aim at the core: they are equalizers of men. The poor sing, entertain, ridicule, cajole, and sometimes subtly threaten by means of song, rhyme and riddle, reminding those that they sing to that this is the time of the year to share in their good fortune. At some points in our history, it got quite ugly at times, with bands of the Callithumpians actually threatening and then breaking into the houses of the rich in order to get their Bowl of Beer. Some would call the tradition Social Extortion; today it is far more gentle and benign, and it is called Caroling.

Books

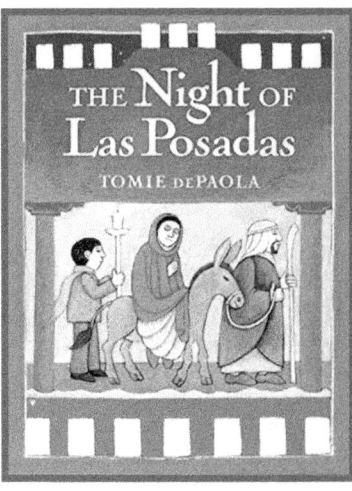

The Legend ofOld Befana by
Tomie dePaola
ISBN-9780152438173

The Legend of the Poinsettia
by Tomie dePaola
ISBN-9780698115675

The Night of Las Posadas by
Tomie dePaola
ISBN-13:9780698119017

298

Day 11

REMEMBRANCES

 hese are the stories I collected from my friends, family and people I met while traveling overseas, most notably from the Coalition Forces in Camp Bucca, Iraq. These stories are their most favorite memories of their Winter Celebrations and Traditions.

Memories of Twelfth Night

IS2 Haurilick
Compound 16
NPDB4
Camp Bucca, Iraq

I grew up in numerous European countries thanks to my Army father and my Scottish mother. So I got to observe and participate in several traditions at Christmas time that are not normally observed here in the States, St. Nicholas Day on December 5th was one and the other was Twelfth Night. On twelfth Night, people traditionally would bring out their Christmas trees and greenery that they had decorated the house with and have a huge bonfire.

I don't remember this happening in Germany, but I do remember one year in Vermont that our Church had a Twelfth Night Christmas Tree Bonfire. It wasn't done in the traditional sense; I think rather, it was a unique way to help the Church members get rid of the Christmas trees and have one last hurrah before the dullness of late winter set in.

A bonfire area was set up in the parking lot of St. Andrews and of course, the appropriate fire permits obtained from the Fire Department. People started showing up at twilight and bringing their trees. Mothers brought food and treats and the men brought libations and stories to trade around the fire. The children brought too much energy, and the last of the Christmas sugar highs were used up running around like crazy elves. There was potluck down in the undercroft and Christmas music playing on the stereo, and we were all impatient for the official start of the bonfire.

Shortly after all the men arrived, dressed out in their flannels and work boots, mufflers and flap hats, the Pastor gave a brief blessing and then the stacking began. There is a certain art to stacking a bonfire and even more so when it is sap-filled trees. So of course, every man in the crowd had to give his two cents worth of how it was done right, and boy howdy...when HE was a child, it was done right and it was never done like this… etc. and so forth, you get the picture. Finally and at long last, the fire marshal inspected the pile and gave the go ahead. What a relief!! Finally, the matches were lit, the men positioned and the women, with children on their laps, surrounding the fire in lawn chairs and quilts, held their breaths.

Us kids just wanted to see how high the flames would go and wished the adults would shut up. Whoosh!!! The flames shot up and the crackling began . . . We all cheered and then the evening began. Adults sat in chairs around the fire, kids raced around annoying their parents, screaming and singing. Teenagers flirted and smiled at each other as the boys acted up to catch the attention of the girls.

I don't remember how old I was, but I remember all this, and drinking hot chocolate and eating my Nana's doughnuts, alternately sitting and running around the fire. It was mesmerizing, staring into

those huge flames and listening to the adults tell stories and visit with their neighbors. The night didn't end until the last tree had been fed to the flames and let to die down to glowing embers. I don't think it was done again, or perhaps we moved, I don't recall, but I remember that night. I remember the smell of woodsmoke and pine, hot chocolate and hot casseroles, the sound of children laughing and men rumbling in discussion, the murmurs of women and above all the sound of the cracking fire.

Memories of La Befana

DC1 Danny Trampe
Compound 19 Controller
NPDB4
Camp Bucca, Iraq

From my earliest memories in our household we have celebrated "La Befana," or roughly translated, "the Good Witch". The story of La Befana as translated by my Italian mother is a long tradition amongst European families. Befana is celebrated on what is believed to be the night that the Three Kings arrived at the manger to present the Christ Child with the gifts of gold, incense and myrrh.

Unlike Saint Nicholas, Befana rewards children for their reverence during the Holiday Season. Befana only gives gifts to children who keep the message of the birth as their central focus of Christmas. Befana keeps a close eye on you to make sure you are respectful of your parents and your elders, sort of like an assistant to Santa Claus. Even as we grew older and wiser and came to know that Jolly Old Saint Nick was actually grumpy and tired Father and Mother, my mom always managed to convince us that Befana was real.

Befana's gifts were never huge, typically items easily found at the modern day dollar stores, but they were always appreciated. In my neighborhood, all the other "non-Italian" kids were always wondering what the magical witch was bringing us. The day would continue on like any other with the exception of dinner. Mom would make up a huge batch of pasta for us. On Befana she would forget the "everyday" dishes we would normally use and instead opt for the fine China normally reserved for guests. No special recipes were required for mom, she always knew what was on the menu:

- Pasta with her own sauce—canned months ago

- Meatballs—special Italian spices added

- Garlic bread—normally burnt (she could never get that part right)

- Red wine (adults only)

- Tiramisu dessert—store bought (Mom said it takes too long to make herself)

302

RECIPES

ere I add recipes for the day: both traditional and from a different country/culture. I hope that you will try a few of these recipes and perhaps incorporate them into your family traditions.

Yule Log Cake

The Yule cake tradition evolved from the actual Yule Log itself. When people moved from country to town and fireplaces went away, people wanted to remember. So of course the French (I think) came up with a cake recipe to carry on the history. I cannot find a recipe simple enough to actually try and not muff up to the extent that I couldn't recommend it to you. So, I will simply give you my friend Marcy's nice and simple, but effective, "cheat." I will, at a later date, put in a proper Yule Log recipe for you but for now, here she is:

Directions

Buy a roll cake at the Grocery store, any flavor will do. At the same time buy a can of frosting, white or chocolate. Also, pick up some powdered sugar and some maraschino cherries.

Once you get the cake home, place it on the platter on which you intend to serve it. Frost with your choice of frosting. Using a fork, make wavy lines up and down the length of the log to simulate bark. Place cherries on one end to simulate berries. Gently sift a fine coating of powdered sugar over the length of the log. The white "snow" shows up better on chocolate bark.

Spicy Nuts

My mom and dad like to golf. When they retired and moved to the South, they of course placed themselves strategically near a golf course. Dad goes more than mom, and it was on one of his "walks" that he discovered a whole lot of pecan trees on the course and a whole lot of unattended pecans UNDER the trees. So, on his next "walk," he brought a bag and collected a few nuts. That became a tradition and now, whenever dad brings home golf nuts, we, my mom and I, plan to make Frosted Christmas Nuts. Again, not a huge fan of nuts, but frosted pecans? I make an exception. Spicy foods are a traditional aspect of the 12th Night celebration.

Ingredients

- 2 egg whites

- 1 cup sugar

- ½ tsp. cinnamon

- ¼ tsp. salt

- 4-5 cups pecans

- ½ cup margarine

Directions

Beat egg whites until fluffy. Stir in sugar, cinnamon and salt. Stir in the nuts until coated. In a shallow baking pan, melt margarine. Add nuts to the baking pan.

Bake at 325°F for 45–60 minutes, stirring every 10–15 minutes. Remove from the oven when nuts are lightly browned, and all the margarine has been absorbed.

Let cool. Store in plastic containers in the fridge, or you can freeze them too.

Caramel Apple Loki

I got this recipe from a witch I met in Iraq. We had a large number of Pagan's in our Unit, believe it or not, and just like the Christians and the Jews, they had a meeting night for prayers and support. I went when I could make my night off match up with the meeting night because they were a fascinating group of people. There were all types of Pagans in that group. Some self-professed witches, a few general Pagans, one Celtic Druid and one gloomy-looking guy who said he was a Satanist, but he wasn't sure.

In any case, Elizabeth was kind enough to share one of her Coven's favorite drinks for the Winter Solstice celebration with me. I am not a Pagan, but I find the history of their religion very interesting, and my meetings with this group were very informative and fun. They let me come even though I just professed interest not intent. After our first mortar attack, they placed stones of protection outside our living trailer, and I have to admit, it brought me comfort.

Ingredients

- 1 fifth (bottle) of Everclear

- ¾ of a 5th bottle of Apple Pucker

- ½ cup caramel topping

- 1 bottle vanilla extract

- 5 cups sugar

- 1 gallon glass jar

Directions

Place all the ingredients in the glass jar. Top off a few cups of water. Ferment for a minimum of four hours, a few days is better. Place it in a cool, dark area.

For Loki's Revenge, use Apple Pucker in place of the Everclear; it is a sweeter drink.

Apple Nog

This recipe is the exactly the same as the Chocolate Eggnog on Day Twelve. Just trade out the chocolate for two cups of organic apple cider. You can also cut some apple slices to float on top of the nog while it is in the pitcher or serving bowl.

Ingredients

- 1 (14 oz) can of Eagle Brand Condensed Milk NOT evaporated milk

- 4 eggs

- 3 cups milk

- ½ tsp. vanilla

- dash salt

- ½ cup bourbon or brandy

- ¼ tsp nutmeg or cinnamon

Directions

In a large bowl, beat the eggs. Gradually add in the remaining ingredients. Whip for a few minutes to ensure a good mixture. Chill, garnish with apples, nutmeg or cinnamon. Refrigerate.

Wassail

Ingredients

- ½ gallon of apple juice

- 2 cups of cranberry juice

- 1 cups of orange juice

- ½ medium-sized orange, use peels in strips

- ½ medium-sized lemon, use peels in strips

- 2 cinnamon sticks

- 2 whole cloves

- 2 allspice berries

Directions

Combine all ingredients into slow cooker on LOW for 4 hours. Strain and return to the slow cooker to keep warm while serving.

PUZZLES

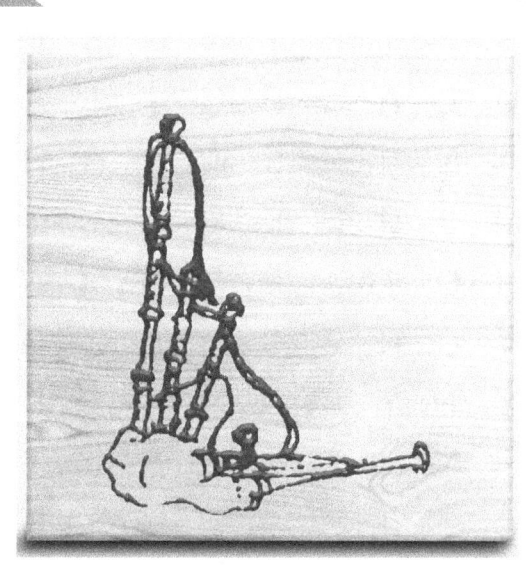

```
J A M E S T H E Y O U N G E R B W E F
S A M O H T O M Z P T Y I E K A Y F J
R O O P I J O E P I L I H P C G N Y R
T S I R I S U Q O A E E H C U P E G W
F G R E D L E E H T S E M A J I X N R
O N W E H T T A M E E T S S E P H I R
P I P E R S P I P I N G S P C E S L S
E K R S X U L A Q E C I T A O N J R P
L E O K I A N D R E W R R R A P E I A
T E I L P M J U D E S O I T M M T K E
T R H Q Y N O T A P L G H W I L S S C
A H C N U V C N A S G A Z O U L T E K
B T L H L Y F I B D N S E S C E V Q E
D R E O D H N U F I B A L T H A Z A R
Y D M J K C T J E P A M X K H H O Z X
R M M I L F H L D I S C I P L E S A U
```

Andrew	**Balthazar**	**Carols**	**Disciples**
James the Elder	**John**	**Matthew**	**Nathanael**
Philip	**Simon**	**Spain**	**Three Kings**
Bagpipe	**Battle**	**Caspar**	
James the Younger	**Jude**	**Melchior**	
Piper's Piping	**Skirling**	**Thomas**	

CROSS STITCH DESIGN-YULE

These are designs for cross stitch patterns that you can use for ornaments, throws, or dishcloths. They are a work in progress, so if you can improve upon the design, go for it!! The patterns might not all be up by Christmas Time, so if the patterns aren't up this week, check back again.

312

Day 11

COLORING PAGES/RED WORK DESIGN - COLORING PAGES/RED WORK DESIGN - LA BEFANA / ITALY

These are designs that can be used either for coloring pages for children or copied and transferred to cloth for Redwork for quilts. I kept the lines simple for both those reasons. Many of the designs have dots on them to show where to sew miniature bells or gold beads on them to represent jingle bells.

La Befana
Italy

3 - Italy - La Befana

In Italy, Santa Claus is called Babbo Natale, and he has eight reindeers as well. Their names are: Cometa, Ballerina, Fulmine, Donnola, Freccia, Saltarello, Donato, Cupido (Comet, Dancer, Dasher, Prancer, Vixen, Donder, Blitzen, Cupid). It is traditionally a more reserved and solemn holiday than the US observes, as La Befana is still much more popular. La Befana is an old woman who delivers gifts to children throughout Italy on January 5th or the Eve of Epiphany, in the same way that Santa Claus or Saint Nicholas would do.

This Italian gift-giving spirit is also known as Saint Befana, La Vecchia (the Old Woman), and La Strega (the Witch).[1] When La Befana visits the children of Italy on the night of January 5th, she fills their socks with toys and presents if they are good, or a lump of coal or dark candy if they are bad. The child's family typically leaves a small glass of wine and a plate with a few morsels of food for La Befana to eat when she visits.

The legend goes that when she was told by the Three Kings that the baby Jesus was born, she told her visitors she was too busy and delayed visiting the baby. She missed the Star, lost her way, and has been flying around ever since, leaving presents at every house with children in case He is there. She is usually portrayed as a smiling, kindly old lady wearing a shawl and carrying her basket of candy, gifts and food, riding a broomstick through the air, and entering the house through the window or the chimney.

316

TWELVE DRUMMERS DRUMMING

Drums, as we know them, did not exist until after the crusades. Before that, the Europeans had the tambourine. Drums were used first in war, then by the town watchman, know as "the wait" to make announcements and then became part of caroling from door to door.

rums, as we know them, did not exist before the Crusades. Before that the Europeans had the tambourine. Drums were first used in war and then by the town watchman, known as "The Wait," to make announcements, and then became a part of caroling from door to door.

Also known as Three Kings Day or the Feast of the Epiphany.

318

BIBLICAL INTERPRETATION

The Twelve Drummers drumming symbolize the twelve points of belief in the apostle's creed.

The Twelve Drummers Drumming symbolizes the twelve points of belief in the Apostles Creed.

320

ANOTHER CULTURE'S WINTER CELEBRATION

3 kings Day Jan 6 Spain

Three Kings Day

    The twelve days of Christmas end with the Feast of Epiphany also called "The Adoration of the Magi." Celebrated on January 6th, it is known as the day of the Three Kings (or wise men/magi) Kaspar, Melchior and Balthasar. According to an old legend based on a Bible story, these three kings saw, on the night when Christ was born, a bright star, followed it to Bethlehem and found the Christ child and presented Him with gold, frankincense, and myrrh.

This Holiday is celebrated more so than Christmas in most Latin American countries and in some European households. Traditionally there were three Magi, probably from the fact of three gifts, even though the biblical narrative never says how many Magi came. In some cultures, especially Hispanic and Latin American culture, January 6th is observed as Three Kings Day, or simply the Day of the Kings: *el Dia de los Reyes,* and in the Dutch: *Drei Koningen Dag.* Even though December 25th is celebrated as Christmas in these cultures, January 6th is often the day for giving gifts. In some places, it is traditional to give Christmas gifts for each of the Twelve Days of Christmas.

Books

Three Kings and a Star by Fred Crump
ISBN-9781932715521

The Firefly Star by Sandra Robbins
ISBN-1882601-68-8

N is for Navidad by Susan Middleton Elya, Merry Banks
ISBN-13: 9780811852050

Bienvenidos! To a celebration of Christmas, Latino-style! From the ngel (angel) hung above the door to the zapatos (shoes) filled with grass for the wise men's camels, each letter in this festive alphabet introduces children to a Spanish word.

REMEMBRANCES

rummers Drumming

hese are the stories I collected from my friends, family, and people I met while traveling overseas, most notably from the Coalition Forces in Camp Bucca, Iraq. These stories are their most favorite memories of their Winter Celebrations and Traditions.

Melissa C.
Comptroller, Compound 19
Camp Bucca, Iraq

I grew up in a small town in PA. Our family was also small, eleven people including grandparents. Each year for Thanksgiving, we would make homemade stuffing the night before and have a slumber party with our cousins at my Mimi's house (grandma). Then we would wake up and help her cook. After dinner, we would all play Trivial Pursuit. Mimi always tried to whisper answers, but everyone always heard them. When the first snowfall came, we put up the tree, music and all. Even if the snow came in September, up went the tree.

When I joined the Navy, the tradition continued. My first duty station was Sicily. My mom sent me a little tree in August with all the fixings, telling me it had snowed at home. So I put up the tree. No matter where I am, when the first snow falls in PA, my mom calls me and my daughters get so excited, because then the tree will go up and to them, Christmas is just around the corner.

Day 12

RECIPES

ere I add recipes for the day: both traditional and from a different country/culture. I hope that you will try a few of these recipes and perhaps incorporate them into your family traditions.

Chocolate Eggnog and Churritos

This is a basic Eggnog recipe to which you can add almost any flavor. For a nice rich chocolate flavor, add 8 ounces of melted semi-sweet chocolate chips or a few packets of Hot Chocolate mix. One of my friends swears by one can of Hershey's Syrup. Try all three and see what works for you.

Ingredients

- 1 (14 oz.) can of Eagle Brand Condensed Milk(NOT evaporated milk)

- 4 eggs

- 3 cups milk

- ½ tsp. vanilla

- dash salt

- ½ cup Bourbon or brandy

- ¼ tsp nutmeg or cinnamon

- 8 oz. Chocolate chips/1 can hershey's Syrup/3-4 Hot Chocolate packets

Directions

In a large bowl, beat the eggs. Gradually add in the remaining ingredients. Whip for a few minutes to ensure a good mixture. Chill. Garnish with nutmeg or cinnamon. Refrigerate.

Churritos

This is an extremely good snack when eaten with hot chocolate. I never knew cinnamon went so well with chocolate.

Ingredients

- 2 cups of water

- 1 ½ tsp. salt

- 2 cups all-purpose flour

- 1 tsp. ground cinnamon

- 1 cup sugar

- Canola oil for frying

Directions

In a saucepan, bring water and salt to a boil. Gradually add flour, stirring quickly until a ball forms. Once the ball is fully formed, remove it the saucepan and put in a floured work surface. Allow to cool for a few minutes, then start kneading it for about 3-4 minutes. Put it into a pastry bag with a 3/8 inch star tip.

In a separate bowl, mix the cinnamon and sugar.

Use a deep-fat fryer if you have one. Otherwise, pour oil into a deep skillet to a depth of 2 plus inches. Heat it up 'til a drop of water sizzles in it. Then it's ready.

Pipe the dough directly into oil, using kitchen shears to snip off lengths every 3–4 inches. Fry only a few at a time to ensure they don't fry together. Remove from oil with a slotted spoon and paper towel dry. Toss in the cinnamon/sugar mixture and serve warm with hot chocolate or chocolate eggnog.

If you don't want to be bothered with the mixing and the measuring, they do sell a box of Churrito mix called Tres Estrellas, the Three Stars brand, at most Mexican Grocery stores. They also sell Abuelitas Hot Chocolate discs, which have cinnamon in them and are really good. They also sell premade churritos but that kinda takes out the fun of dropping dough into hot sizzling fat and almost getting burned. Screwing up while cooking is half the fun!!

Mayan Fire Pie

There is this bar in Raleigh that is called the Tir Na Nog. They had the most awesome Sunday Brunch with live Irish music and a Mimosa to die for. They also have a unique pie on the menu that I have been assured it is a best seller. I didn't believe Pete at first. Pete is the owner. But, as I said that, literally as the words had just left my mouth and were floating on the air, a waitress arrived and delivered said pie to the table directly next to myself and my friend Phronsie. I looked at it. It looked good. Really good. But, as I have said previously, ANYTHING is good dipped in chocolate. Apparently, even bacon. Yup. You heard me. Chocolate Bacon Pie. Hmm …

Still wasn't convinced. But, I went to the State Fair this year and guess what was one of the featured items? Besides deep fried pickle chips that is, (I swear, deep-fried pickle chips, and they are GOOD!) and deep fried butter! I didn't even want to think about that one. Wait for it. Chocolate bacon on a stick. Uh huh.

AND then . . . A few days later, I went to World Market (I love that store) and I bought a candy bar that is seventy-two percent pure cacao chocolate AND bacon. A bacon candy bar. Nothing burps better than bacon except for bacon and chocolate.

Why on earth am I going on about bacon and chocolate? 'cause here is a pie that has both. Chocolate pie with a zing with bacon brittle. The zing is cayenne pepper and before you think I have had one too many, the ancients who discovered chocolate used to mix it with peppers, and grind it up, and drink it as a cold drink. Sugar wasn't added for many hundreds of years.

Give it a shot.

Ingredients

- Pre-made Graham Cracker Crumb Crust
- ¼ cup cornstarch
- ½ cup granulated sugar
- 1/8 tsp. salt
- 1 cup whole milk
- 2 large egg yolks, beaten
- 8 oz. of semi sweet chocolate
- 2 tsp. of Cayenne pepper
- 1 tsp. cinnamon
- 1 tsp. vanilla
- 1 cup Cool Whip

Directions

Mix cornstarch, sugar, and salt in a saucepan. Add a quarter cup of milk and whisk until smooth. Turn the heat to medium and slowly add the remaining milk and egg yolks, stirring constantly. The mixture will thicken quite fast, so don't turn your back on it. When the mixture is thick enough, take it off the stove and stir in the chocolate and the spices. When the chocolate is melted, add the vanilla. Pour into a mixing bowl to cool.

When it has cooled a little, add a cup of Cool Whip. Mix well. Spread mixture on the bottom of Graham Cracker crust. Top with the remaining Cool Whip and then add a few pieces of bacon brittle for garnish.

Bacon Brittle

This is really yummy, even though it DOES look like a cat hairball at first.

Ingredients

- 1/2 cup sugar

- ½ cup light corn syrup

- 1 Tbsp. packed brown sugar

- 1 Tbsp. unsalted butter, softened

- 1 tsp salt

- ¼ cup Bacon that has been cut into small bits,

DO NOT use Bacon Bits

Directions

Line the baking sheet with parchment paper. Mix the first five ingredients together, and then add the bacon bits. Drop spoonfuls onto the parchment paper, spacing an inch apart. Preheat oven to 350°F and bake it for about eighteen minutes. The whole mixture will merge into one big lake of bacon and sugar. That's ok. Remove from the oven and let cool. Smash into pieces for garnish. It looks gross at first but OH MY!! YUM!!!

Note: Be careful to refrigerate if not serving immediately, the brittle will get gooey and soft if you leave it out on the counter too long.

PUZZLES

```
L D A E X B U W A T C H M A N T R U
I R S O A M D E G L I T D U F F D O
J U T E Q M F D N M A F M M P E P W
D M N U O Z N N F C O V S Q W A O F
Z M I D Q T D T M B M I N D K A L T
W E O E L U S W S E D A S U R C E W
E R P T R T R L O E U Y Z O T U T E
U S E H M L N D D Y M E I F R U O L
R D V E D E E R C S E L T S O P A F
O R L W E N U T A M B O R I N E O T
P U E A K M O F J B E R I F N O B H
E M W I A D R T E D V E X T P J D N
A M T T V M W U G O L E L U Y I M I
N I E D W L L V Q M F W R X P L A G
S N T C E R G N I L O R A C J I F H
P G I W E J U C T E E P N I W N T
```

Apostles Creed	Caroling	Drummers Drumming	Side Drum
Tamborine	Twelfth Night	Watchman	
Bonfire	Crusades	Europeans	
The Wait	Twelve Points	Yule Log	

Day 12

CROSS STITCH DESIGN - THREE KINGS / LATIN AMERICA

 hese are designs for cross stitch patterns that you can use for ornaments, throws or dishcloths. They are a work in progress, so if you can improve upon the design, go for it!!! The patterns might not all be up by Christmas Time, so if the pattern isn't up this week, check back again.

333

334

COLORING PAGES/RED WORK DESIGN- THREE KINGS / LATIN AMERICA

hese are designs that can be used either for coloring pages for children or copied and transferred to cloth for Redwork for quilts. I kept the lines simple for both those reasons. Many of the designs have dots on them to show where to sew miniature bells or gold beads on them to represent jingle bells.

Three Kings
Latin America

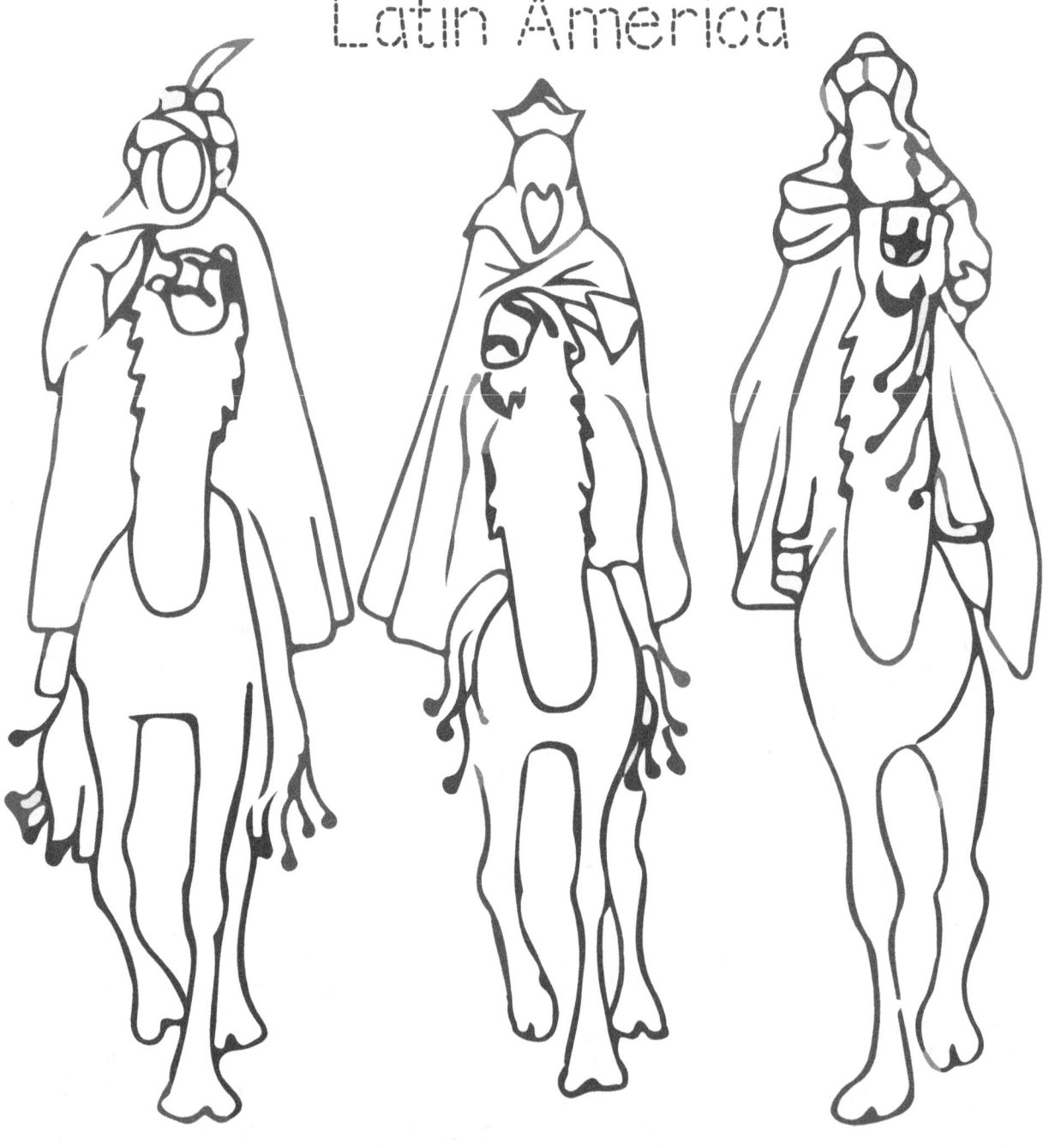

6 - Latin America - Three Kings

In the Spanish-speaking parts of the world, many cultures celebrate Three Kings Day more so than Christmas Day. They celebrate the Magi on January 6, Day of Epiphany, the day immediately following the Twelve Days of Christmas. They are called "los Reyes Magos de Oriente", also "Los Tres Reyes Magos" and "Los Reyes Magos," and they receive wish letters from children and magically bring them gifts on the night before Epiphany. Each one of the Magi is supposed to represent one different continent, Europe (Melchior), Asia (Kaspar) and Africa (Balthasar). According to tradition, the Magi come from the Orient on their camels to visit the houses of all the children. Like their American counterparts, the children leave food and drink for the Kings, as well as the camels, as this is the only night of the year the camels supposedly eat.

Almost every Latin American town organizes a parade or a Cabalgatas in the evening, in which the kings and their servants parade and throw sweets to the children and it is called Las Calvacades de los Tres Reyes.

Another tradition in Europe is the writing of the King's initials, along with the year number split around them, as a form of a blessing for the New Year, above the main door of the home in chalk. For example, **"20 * K + M + B * 11"** would be written for 2011. The writing is done by the so-called Sternsinger (star singers), elementary aged school children dressed up as the Magi, carrying the star and singing traditional Christmas Carols. It is part of the Sternsinger tradition that one of the three children will blacken his or her face with soot, in memory of the legend that one of the Magi was of African origin.

Bibliography

Clancy, R. Best-loved Christmas Carols. Edited by Ronald M. Clancy. Illustrated edition. Volume 1 of Millennia collection. Christmas Classics, 2000, p. 75. ISBN: 0615114601, 9780615114606.

Comfort, D. Just Say Noel: A History of Christmas from the Nativity to the Nineties. Illustrated edition. Simon and Schuster, 1995. ISBN: 0684800578, 9780684800578.

Dreary, T. and Brown, M. Horrible Christmas (Horrible Histories). Scholastic Inc.; Reprint edition, 2000. ISBN-10:0439997984, ISBN-13: 978-0439997980.

Freeman, M. Kindling the Celtic Spirit: Ancient Traditions to Illumine Your Life Through the Seasons. HarperOne, 1st ed., December 26, 2000. ISBN-10:006251685X; ISBN-13: 978-0062516855.

Hervey, T. K. The Book of Christmas. Independently Published, 2019. ISBN-10: 170306089X; ISBN-13: 978-1703060898.

Israel, E. Celebrate the Winter Holidays: Sensational Activities & Helpful Background Information That Help Kids Learn About & Appreciate Five Important Holidays. Scholastic Teaching Resources, January 1, 2001. ISBN-10: 0439073456; ISBN-13: 978-0439073455.

Lester, M. Why Does Santa Wear Red?: ...and 100 Other Christmas Curiosities Unwrapped! Simon and Schuster, 2007. ISBN-10: 1440516561; ISBN-13: 978-1440516566.

Matthews, J. Winter Solstice: The Sacred Traditions of Christmas. Theosophical Publishing House, 1998. ISBN: 9780835607698.

Miles, C. Christmas Customs and Traditions, Their History and Significance. Illustrated, reprint, revised edition. Dover books on anthropology: Political and social science. Courier Corporation, 1976. ISBN-10: 0486233545; ISBN-13: 978-0486233543.

Morrison, D. Yule: A Celebration of Light and Warmth. Illustrated edition. Volume 2 of Holiday Series. Llewellyn Worldwide, 2000. ISBN-10: 1567184960; ISBN-13: 978-1567184969.

Nissenbaum, S. The Battle for Christmas: A Cultural History of America's Most Cherished Holiday. Knopf Doubleday Publishing Group, 2010. ISBN-10: 0307760227; ISBN-13: 978-0307760227.

Pfeffer, W. The Shortest Day: Celebrating the Winter Solstice. Illustrated by Jesse Reisch. Illustrated edition. Dutton Children's Books, 2003. ISBN-10: 0525469680; ISBN-13: 978-0525469681.

Remson, A. Where Did Christmas Come From? Berkley Publishing Group, 1996. ISBN-10: 0399522476; ISBN-13: 978-0399522475.

Renterghem, T. V. When Santa was a Shaman: The Ancient Origins of Santa Claus & the Christmas Tree. Illustrated edition. Llewellyn Publications, 1995. ISBN-10: 156718765X; ISBN-13: 978-1567187656.

Rouse, J. M. History, Legends & Folklore of Christmas. Writers Club Pr, January 1, 2001. ISBN-10: 059520080X; ISBN-13: 978-0595200801.

Websites

🌐 www.abdicate.net

🌐 www.angelfire.com

🌐 www.astrosociety.org

🌐 www.belief.net

🌐 www.byrum.org/misc/christmas/origin.html

🌐 www.carols.org.uk

🌐 www.christianitytoday.com

🌐 www.cresourcei.org

🌐 www.discoverhongkong.com/eng/heritage/festivals/he_fest_wint.jhtml

🌐 www.dltk-holidays.com/xmas/12/twelve.htm

🌐 www.fardos.net (Nasif Kayed)

🌐 www.familydharma.pulelehuadesign.com

🌐 www.geocities.com

🌐 www.geocities.com/Paris/Parc/1486/festival/cny.html

🌐 www.hoaxbusters.com

🌐 www.ing.com

🌐 www.indiafairs.dgreetings.com

🌐 www.inventors.about.com

🌐 www.islamtomorrow.com

🌐 www.islaml.org

🌐 www.korova.com

🌐 www.kuro5hin.org

🌐 www.museum.org

🌐 www.nomadiournaltrips.com

🌐 www.olivercromwell.org

🌐 www.parstimes.com

🌐 www.reacheverychild.com

🌐 www.religioustolerance.org/winter_solstice.htm

🌐 www.santaynezchumash.org

🌐 www.siutao.com

🌐 www.siutao.com/id/ibd/ibd_yuanxiao.shtml

🌐 www.souledout.org/festivals

🌐 www.spkmandarin.cbn.com.sg

🌐 www.spkmandarin.cbn.com.sg/spkmandarin/festival/dongzhi.htm

🌐 www.stnicholascenter.org

🌐 www.symantec.com

🌐 www.truthorfiction.com/rumors/t/twelvedaysofchristmas.htm

🌐 www.vmyths.com

🌐 www.webster.com

🌐 www.whysilamd.com

🌐 www.wisdomportal.com/Christmas/Notes-12DaysOfChristmas.html

🌐 www.quotidianmeander.blogspot.com

PUZZLE 1 Page 44

```
Q D Y D R Y H Y W Z S P C J
D N O W Z E Y E C B E Y U E
F A O R P E O H O A T W G S
R L C E O D R X R P U D U U
U I G J N R I N V C I H S S
I N E A S N C K R R G C P C
T E F T G X C O T A C K W H
D C M D V I D R H S O C O R
E A A L H W A H I R M M G I
S Y N E H P E T S T N I A S
E G I R K A U E L Z M M C T
M S U A L C A T N A S A R E
```

PUZZLE 2 Page 72

```
F T E S T A M E N T S A E N
A D O N G Z H I Q Y I D M M
I R M O T H E R S N I G H T
T A M E T C C E L C F T R X
H T U R T L E D O V E S Y P
F O R U W C C I O A C P A
U N O O M H T N E V E L E Y
L G E B Y I Y P I J W G P O
N X K S G N I L P M U D V B
E I D W D A L O V E E R X
S B F W Z J C L S E O N I
S M A R I T A L B L I S S N
```

PUZZLE 3 Page 94

```
P U N P U O I P E P E T C Z V
I U E O J Q E G I P D U O M Z
W A T E R M E L O N A R I U V
M U T D M S F R E T S O O R J
S E H U T U N G O O D L U C K
H V O W P O M E G R A N A T E
T O P O E G Y D H U H S O E D
X P E E Y E O I C H T T O I E
A D L A Y E B A H S C G I X M
W H I T E H E N S I A N A A K
D O O H R E H T O M P R E U F
F U B E B P U C B U I S D R L
A S O O B Y C H A R I T Y U F
```

PUZZLE 4 Page 126

```
F E A S T O F F O O L S Z Y
A S L U K E W R E I A I U Y
M A R K D T F E U I I A E I
A T D S L E P S O G R U O F
T U S D R I B Y L L O C J F
T R L A S R E V E R E L O R
H N D D Y A A N N L C U H N
E A O D I E V E B I P Y N N
W L V R D A U E A O Y R X N
I I D S E W J C A N E O Z F
E A B L A C K B I R D P I E
```

PUZZLE 5 Page 150

```
P W Z M E H R O C P Y E G O G G P U
E I U O I K O U H M D K E E U Q A G
U M A N S F A L L F R O M G R A C E
M W D I E S M E O Y A D E M I B A F
Y U F I V E G O L D E N R I N G S R
R I N G N E C K E D P H E A S A N T
M R D F I V E T E S T A M E N T S M
R K O A W S F D P M R R O M M N Y O
T Y G I E A A O Q G A E C R A Z F F
E V R L I H U C F A V U R L M A T E
R F E A L A S R F U Z Q Y M C J S I
E U E W A T T R E L I N Q D E N N O
F Q K I Z F E S A A O O U Q A P A U
Z D S D B D S E C O G C W K T I M O
X O L E I B E M U R B S A U B H O D
W D O E V R D N I P C O Z O D S R N
```

PUZZLE 6 Page 176

```
D Q T X A S O L A R Y E A R K U W
Y V E I G G S O T N K L Y D P N Q
J C Z H T R I B E R Y M T X E S R
B A O I N H E R E D M G C B H E A
N E W Y E A R S E V E P V Y G O Z
E T O P F E R T I L I T Y G U P A
I E E D E H J C E M R I A A I Y I
H V D T H A F M W Q E D C O M X V
C H A C O C A N Y O N O F D R G V
C V S A F S O P O U H Y A N Q C
D I E R I G E E S E A L A Y I N G
S I X D A Y S O F C R E A T I O N
U X A I E M Y O V N W E S O O G D
R C C R J I S P U E B L O C O I C
U O M A A U S M N P F I G N O P P
```

PUZZLE 7 Page 204

```
O Y I U A W A S S A I L U J A M A A A
S T E E I U A D L R O W T I R I P S L
T I M R O I M W D H S E F D U F Y Y I
F L U M I F I R S T F O O T I N G A K
I A S K S R J A P S M V S A I B E C E
G T I A Y U U R E V E R E N C E O A Z
N R P R P S W A N S A S W I M M I N G
E O C U R P Q L O E G A R U O C N C U
V M F Y Y U L K U J I C H A G U L I A
E M K N O W L E D G E U A I K M Y N S
M S I E O U K C G S N M Z N U K N O N H
V F E A I I F Y E O N A U M O N B F Y
E O Y T L A Y O R J A M M L H T A N I T
N R E G A B E A W I B J L R Y X W U Z
I W I S D O M K C A T N E M E G D U J
A U N D E R S T A N D I N G H O Y H O
```

PUZZLE 8 Page 228

```
S E M I T L A V E I D E M O N M
H J K M F I V E C A N D L E S B
I I O G N L M G N V P A M N O N
M A I D S A M I L K I N G E U F
S A I N T L U C I A I M Y D R U
T T U I O M C D T S W G U E T U
L W H O D G U X S N J T A W C R
T I I R A L V Q C H J Y K S H U
H E A D W R E A T H R F U G E P
T N U O M E H T N O N O M R E S
K G M T C E A L I D Y T U M S Q
K S W O N S D C A J T R R J E A
C T R L U S S E R K A T Z C B E
E I G H T B E A T I T U D E S I
```

PUZZLE 9 Page 252

```
N A P E P F B A Q E U E V O L N M A L S I A B T Z
F R U I T S O F T H E H O L Y S P I R I T X N G P
S Q C P T Q N P N A L U R O U N D D A N C E S L E
E T R Q N A S P R I N G P L A N T I N G M T N S E
X C N S E H S A E A A I Y I B Q M E N U A E G P
H N A C K V E L N C A B Y O Q R X J E D D H N G E
X O Y E H F A B P O T U W T D B P T O Y E I E H N
I Y L E P I E C P T A L Z G B U H H F Y C N R E R
A G R L M O D Q J I P J U R F G U D Y N T Q E X U
L A M A Y O D U U K M P P D I A Q L A L E R K U I
S R O J V E I S M O U J J L Q U E D E Z G D P W B
N E J Q A S H D D C V I N M G C E T D E T Q Z
D V B S U Y I O L P I E O T N E E H E G C A M M E
G N I R J S E U L C L Y H A S A V E B E Z C A W
T A T O Y S J O P A U R R D S R E Y O Z I U W P Y
H D N K F B J W U D H E A F I B D N T L I J M M X
D A T U X A Y J S R P L J T M S F D S I F N B Y I
Y M P U W Y I E R M I C Y R D J Z E P J R G P R A
E A Z M T R E I E I S J J O R A V E O B M U O S V
P R F B I W I T E U F Y D E E C N E I T A P S X
D R K P S S E V K N N M S S S E N K E E M A O M S
I L S I Q S O R Y F H O D R U T T F I V F D R S L
```

PUZZLE 10 Page 278

```
M O R R I S D A N C E R S R F V
F E R T I L I T Y W A R T F R O
G N I P A E L A S D R O L F W S
S E C N A D G N I P A E L A U I
T E N C O M M A N D M E N T S E
M O R R I S H D A N C E R S I H
Z E A C I X H P F T E S H I A N
U I S N M C U O R D C P M D M N
A E P A E F E N Y I T I I T D U
D R E I D E L S E T E N Z N Q K
A F R I C A M R Y N A N T I P K
E O O A M R E A N T N I B A N A
L H E U G B D G V A U N L S M H
I M J D W T G O S E J G O P C A
```

PUZZLE 11 Page 310

```
J A M E S T H E Y O U N G E R B W E F
S A M O H T O M Z P T Y I E K A Y F J
R O O P I J O E P I L I H P C G N Y R
T S I R I S U Q O A E E H C U P E G W
F G R E D L E E H T S E M A J I X N R
O N W E H T T A M E E T S S E P H I R
P I P E R S P I P I N G S P C E S L S
E K R S X U L A Q E C I T A Q N J R P
L E O K I A N D R E W R R R A P E I A
T E I L P M J U D E S O I T M M T K E
T R H Q Y N O T A P L G H W I L L S C
A H C N U V C N A S G A Z O U L T E K
B T L H L Y F I B D N S E S C E V Q E
D R E O D H N U F I B A L T H A Z A R
Y D M J K C T E P A M X K H H O Z X
R M M I L F H L D I S C I P L E S A U
```

PUZZLE 12 Page 332

```
L D A E X B U W A T C H M A N T R U
I R S O A M D E G L I T D U F F D O
J U T E Q M F D N M A F M M P E P W
D M N U O Z N N F C O V S Q W A O F
Z M I D Q T D T M B M I N D K A L T
W E O E L U S W S E D A S U R C E W
E R P T R T R L O E U Y Z O T U T E
R U S E H M L N D D Y M E I F R U O L
D V E D E E R C S E L T S O P A O T
O R L W E N U T A M B O R I N E O T
P U E A K M O F J B E R I F N O B T
E M W I A D R T E D V E X T P J D N
A M T T V M W U G O L E L U Y I M I
N I E D W L L V Q M F W R X P L A G
S N T C E R G N I L O R A C J I F H
P G I W E J U C T E E E P N I W N T
```

www.ingramcontent.com/pod-product-compliance
Lightning Source LLC
Chambersburg PA
CBHW081307140626
46546CB00022B/3201